IDENTITY AND CHOREOGRAPHIC PRACTICE

Identity and Choreographic Practice
Published by Serendipity
Serendipity
Room CL00.14, Clephan Building
De Montfort University
The Gateway, Leicester
LE1 9BH

+44 (0) 116 257 7316
info@serendipity-uk.com
www.serendipity-uk.com

Serendipity Artists Movement Limited
Company registration number in England and Wales 07248813
Charity registration number in England and Wales 1160035

CONTENTS

Preface	Pawlet Brookes	02
One Day my Chance will Come	Joan Myers Brown	04

BALLET: THE STRUGGLE FOR VISIBILITY

Black Dancers did Come Up	Delia Barker	10
Looking through the Keyhole: Black dancers in British ballet and the influence of the Dance Theatre of Harlem	Sandie Bourne	14

RE-INSCRIBING AFRICA'S MULTI-DIMENSIONAL AESTHETICS: RECOGNISING THE CRITICAL PLACE OF IMPROVISATION-AS-PERFORMANCE

Moving, Breathing and Being: A Reflection	Francis Angol	24
Embodiology® Neo-African Knowledge Production	Sheron Wray	30
Nuanced Contemporary Ghanaian Identity: Negotiating New Choreographic Barriers and Multifaceted Aesthetics	Terry Bright Kweku Ofosu	36
Freestyle	Kenrick 'H2O' Sandy	46

COLONIAL PASTS: NEW AESTHETICS

The Roots and Routes of African/neo-African Dance Practice and Training	'H' Patten	50
Dance exploration through Reggae Moves	David Hamilton	60
I Found Dance through Flamenco	Yinka Esi Graves	62
Art Dance: An Un-Winnable Battle	Nora Chipaumire	68
Glossary		70
Contributors' Biographies		82

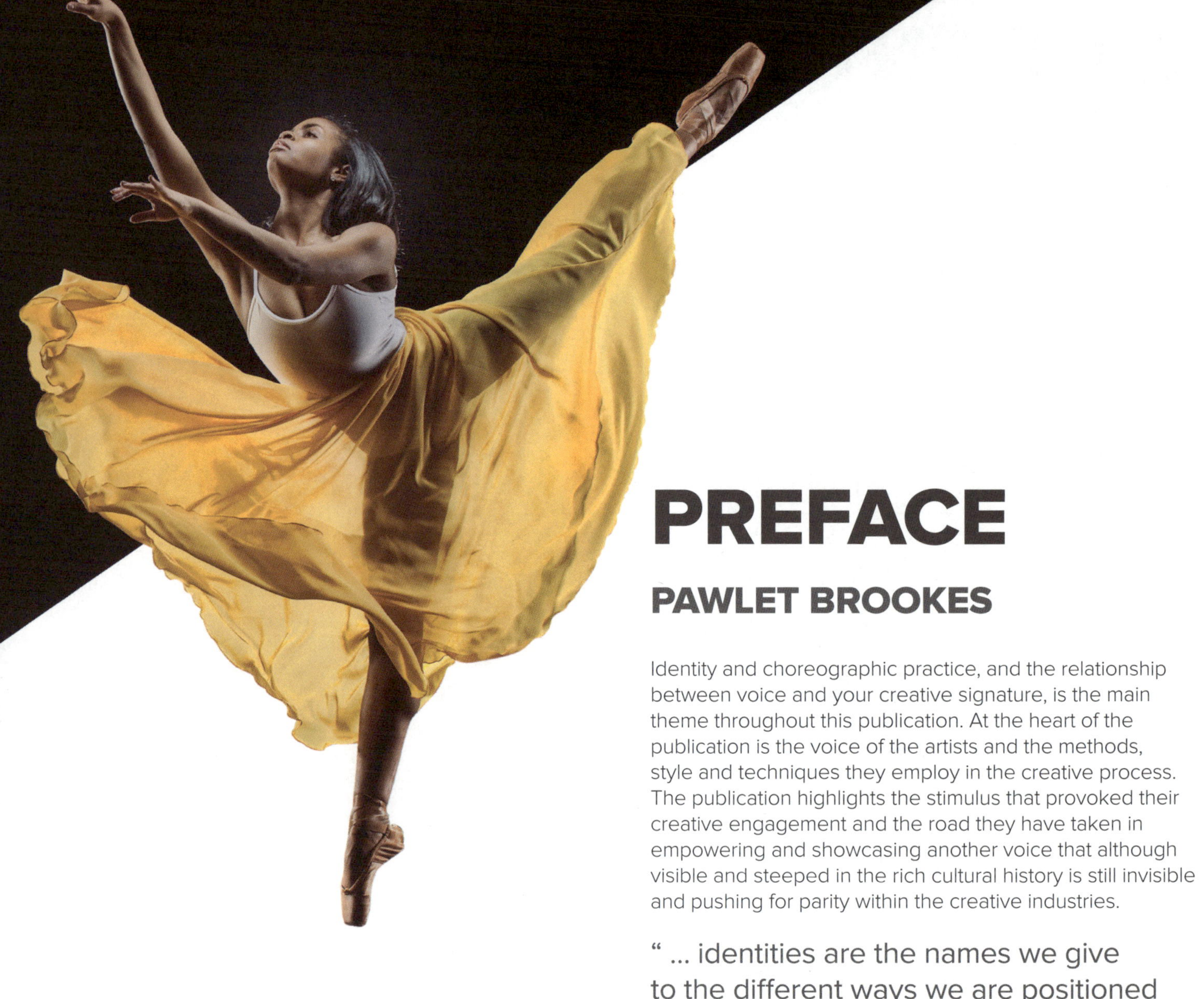

PREFACE

PAWLET BROOKES

Identity and choreographic practice, and the relationship between voice and your creative signature, is the main theme throughout this publication. At the heart of the publication is the voice of the artists and the methods, style and techniques they employ in the creative process. The publication highlights the stimulus that provoked their creative engagement and the road they have taken in empowering and showcasing another voice that although visible and steeped in the rich cultural history is still invisible and pushing for parity within the creative industries.

" ... identities are the names we give to the different ways we are positioned by, and position ourselves within the narratives of the past."

Stuart Hall (1990, p. 225)

The publication opens giving a voice, respect and space to an international portfolio of artists and companies that **Joan Myers Brown** recalls and their role in building an international network and infrastructure around Black dance. The passion and commitment to raising the voice of Black dance internationally has been the driver behind Joan and this commitment is what has been instrumental in changing the face of dance and the profile of Black dancers and choreographers internationally.

"Great dancers are not great because of their technique, they are great because of their passion."

Martha Graham (cited in Gaylin, 2015, p. 17)

Finding a route into practicing dance is a struggle that still prevails, especially when attempting to enter traditionally Eurocentric dance practice, such as classical ballet. **Delia Barker** reflects on searching for Black ballet dancers today, the complex reasons why there are not more Black dancers accessing professional training and the long term commitment needed to find, nurture and support new talent. This may or may not be influenced by the migration of Black British talent that **Sandie Bourne** describes, with a generation of Black British dancers seeking opportunities in the USA with companies such as Dance Theatre of Harlem in the 1970s and 1980s when ballet companies in the UK were not opening their doors to Black dancers. The reality of the situation is that on both sides of the water it is still problematic breaking down the barriers to entry.

However, alternative dance styles and forms are now getting more recognition in that they also require years of training and technique and talent. This is reflected in a collection of papers which explore contemporary African dance, and the influences that have been used to create new technique and practice, with particular reflection on the integral nature of improvisation. **Francis Angol** highlights the role of holistic and internal physical perspective in his own practice through improvisation and somatics. **Sheron Wray** shares the development of her technique Embodiology® and how the principles of African people's practice can pave the way towards new developments, and use of improvisation in performance. **Terry Bright Kweku Ofosu** in turn reflects on the negotiation of creative terrain when it comes to developing new choreography in Ghana. **Kenrick 'H2O' Sandy** describes how improvisation has influenced his own practice, whilst creating a format of dance notation to share his choreography with others.

Identity and Choreographic Practice concludes by bringing together a section that explores how colonial pasts have inspired new aesthetics. **'H' Patten** explores the impact of the transatlantic triangle between African, the Caribbean and the UK, and of African retentions, creolised practices and urban experiences. **David Hamilton** adds to this dialogue with his development of reggae dance. On the other hand, fighting for a presence within Flamenco has led **Yinka Esi Graves** to the discovery that Spain's forgotten Black population and its colonial past has remained largely unacknowledged as an influence on the art form that has always been diverse. **Nora Chipaumire** is unapologetic in her approach as she challenges and negotiates the way Black bodies are presented and the need to decolonise dance practice.

The glossary of practitioners and techniques contextualises the discussion within the publication, providing an insight into the practice that has shaped each contributor's own work, and providing a useful reference. This publication reflects on how each practitioner's journey is different and their resulting choreographic practice is as a result shaped by their experiences, often half by choice, half by chance. But the contributors have all forged a way forward for contemporary dance practice that is reflective of an international dance ecology that offers more choice and new aesthetics when looking at dance.

REFERENCES

Hall, S. (1990) 'Cultural Identity and Diaspora?' in J. Rutherford (ed.) Identity: *Community, Culture, Differen ce*, p. 222-237. London: Lawrence and Wishart.

Gaylin, D. H. (2015) *A Profile of the Performing Arts Industry: Culture and Commerce*. Business Expert Press.

Image Credit: Alexandra Hutchinson. Photographer Richard Calmes.

ONE DAY MY CHANCE WILL COME

JOAN MYERS BROWN

I have "founder's disease", I always say that because I am always starting things and making things happen. I used to say when people asked me to talk that I wish they would ask me to dance. But now that I am older and less inclined to dance, it is the time for me to talk and to share something of my life and career.

I studied ballet all my life and wanted to be the first Black ballerina. That didn't happen and I started working in nightclubs, alongside artists such as Sammy Davis Jr., Cab Calloway and Pearl Bailey. I was lucky as I had a job and I was always dancing. But one morning I woke up and thought, "I don't want to do this anymore, I want to go home," and I thought that maybe if I teach I could give young people the opportunities that I myself had missed.

In 1960 I started the dance school, The Philadelphia School of Dance Arts. I beat up all the kids in my neighbourhood; they came to my dance school and I would beat them to death trying to make them dancers. There was a saying that I put up on the wall *'If I prepare myself one day my chance will come.'* I thought I was preparing kids to dance. Ten years after starting with me when they were six or seven years old, the young people were now sixteen and older. I tried to persuade them to go out and get a job, I sent them to the ballet company in Philadelphia, but they all came back to me. The ballet company didn't want them. That was when I founded PHILADANCO - The Philadelphia Dance Company. I would give them opportunities to perform and get out of town and send them somewhere where they can dance.

Those dancers stayed with me for probably around eight years, and when they left they started going to the Alvin Ailey American Dance Theatre. I started thinking I'm the farm team for Alvin Ailey. Every year someone goes to Ailey Ailey; we currently have about five members in the company who were previously members of PHILADANCO.

The National Endowment for the Arts in America began not long after PHILADANCO was founded, and I was encouraged to apply. I got my first grant of a thousand dollars and at the time I thought I was rich. I thought I would be able to pay my dancers but a thousand dollars doesn't last very long. Fortunately, I was part of a programme called Comprehensive Educational Training Act (CETA), which enabled me to put my dancers on a salary at that time. Then in around 1988 I received a grant for five thousand dollars from an organisation in Philadelphia for artistic development. I was having so many problems and I thought that there must be others in America who were facing similar issues, and maybe there was a way that we could come together and talk about our problems. If we are having the same issues, maybe we can address these.

In 1988, I reached out through Dance USA's Directory to everyone on there that mentioned something about Black, Black African or African American. I sent out a note to them to see if we could organise a meeting and come together. The first meeting that we organised, I thought about six women would turn up and we would talk around my kitchen table. Sixty people showed up. So, we organised another meeting in 1989, and by 1991 we had met several times. We thought that we needed more structure, so we started an organisation the International Association of Blacks in Dance (IABD). IABD is now thirty years old, with conferences in fifteen cities around the USA, and it has also been twice tin Toronto, Canada. It is truly an international organisation, with members coming from around the world, and with trips to the UK we have been reaching out to ensure that dancers of colour from around the world are getting the support and opportunities that they need.

JOAN B. MYERS

In 2016 we held the first Annual Ballet Audition for Women of Colour. We held an audition for 101 dancers from Japan, Haiti, France; girls who wanted to be in ballet. All these ballet directors turned up to look at these dancers and, not only give them jobs, but offer them training. From this twenty-five scholarships were offered and four dancers were invited to company auditions. In 2017 we repeated the audition, capping those auditioning to fifty-seven dancers. Eighteen different company directors came along and The Joffrey Ballet alone gave twenty scholarships. We are trying to make sure that American ballet companies look like America and we will continue to do this until that happens.

When I hold auditions for PHILADANCO, I usually want to hire one or two dancers, but there are always fifty or sixty dancers in the room looking for jobs. My speech to them is always that I am really sorry but that I am unable to hire everyone. I know that they need a job, so I am always about ready to cry. So, I decided to set up a second company PHILADANCO D/2, a training programme, where dancers can take classes and then I can send them out to dance and gain experience. There are always the ladies' auxiliaries, the ladies' sororities and fraternities who want someone to perform at a benefit for them without having to write a cheque. When these groups ask for PHILADANCO to perform, I can send the second company out and the dancers can put on their résumés that they have danced FOR PHILADANCO, and not WITH. With the training and experience, I am able to move many of the dancers from the second company into the first company. In fact, a few years ago I met one of my dancers from the second company in Los Angeles. Her colleagues on her college dance programme couldn't believe how she had already worked with choreographers such as Eleo Pomare, Rod Rogers and Carmen de Lavallade, who she had worked with whilst at PHILADANCO D/2. So, it's an opportunity for them not just to dance, but to meet the masters, the people before them on whose shoulders they stand.

But there is still more work to do. I was talking with an intern earlier this year and I said to her that I needed to call Carmen de Lavallade, and she hadn't even heard of her. I then started to list a number of Black dance artists but she hadn't heard of any of them. She was a dance major at a major institution and she did not know any of these artists; she had not been taught about any of these artists. There is still something missing from our educational system, if you are a dance major and not being taught or trained. I thought, what can I do?

PHILADANCO is the resident company of the Kimmel Centre, which is the major facility in Philadelphia. This is our sixteenth year as the resident company at the centre and we present work twice a year. In December 2017 we presented a programme that reflects on those who have come before, such as Pearl Primus. I have asked Jawole Willa Jo Zollar to do *Walking with Pearl*, and work with Kim Bears-Bailey, who was taught three ballets by Pearl Primus. Then I thought Louis Johnson is 86 years old and very sick, I want to do something while he is still with us. So, we are going to present *Forces of Rhythm*, the ballet he choreographed for Dance Theatre of Harlem. Carmen De Lavallade performed a ballet by Geoffrey Holder. Historically not only will my dancers know, but the people in Philadelphia will know, what our history is.

Then there's Rennie Harris, who took Hip Hop from the street and put it on the stage; he is the foremost Hip Hop artist in the world. Rennie Harris was at IABD and Chuck Davis saw him in Philadelphia and put him on DanceAfrica and took him around the world. I think everyone should know who Rennie Harris is. Fortunately for us, he is from Philadelphia and still rehearses at my studio.

My dance school, in fact I have two schools, has about six hundred children. The four-year olds come up to me and say "I can't wait to grow up to be in PHILADANCO" and I hope I am here to see them when they do grow up to be in PHILADANCO. Previously, there were a lot of really talented young people who could have become dancers, but when they got to twelfth grade they think that they can't dance as a career, instead that they should go to college and become a lawyer, doctor, or teacher. But now that many of the colleges are offering dance majors, there is now the opportunity to go to college and become a dancer, a dance teacher, or a dance historian. There are so many things you can do with dance. So, I took my young people from about the age of twelve and started a youth company, D3 to give them an opportunity to perform. We take them out to perform, in fact on one day in April 17, PHILADANCO, D2 and D3 all had performances at the same time. I had to trust someone and send them out.

In terms of the topic of identity and choreographic practice, the subject of the conference and this publication, I have to admit as someone who does not see herself as a choreographer, that it is a complex and difficult task. As part of a project I produced called *Global Artistry*, I chose to hire choreographers from vastly different backgrounds. Thang Dao was from Vietnam, David Brown was from Jamaica, Francisco Gella was from the Philippines, Aakash Odedra from Leicester in the UK and many multi-faceted choreographers from American communities. So, in terms of my approach to this topic, *how do we define cultural identity?,* is it a place of birth, circumstances of environment or of one's experiences? I can also question what it was about these choreographers that I wanted to add their work to the repertory. Did it have something to do with my multicultural identity? Or was it something incoherent that made me gravitate to their work? What were my expectations when producing this programme? In Philadelphia, every year I try to come up with a programme that will make people see PHILADANCO in a different light. A programme with four different choreographers from four different countries, that surely should be very exciting and enticing for people.

Recently, I have been talking to several choreographers and reviewing existing work in PHILADANCO's repertory. One of the critics of *Global Artistry* said how disappointing it was that in a programme of work that featured so many artists from different backgrounds, that the work did not show any of their own personal reflections and their own cultural experience. Was the critic expecting something more folkloric? We may assume that the choreographers featured were greatly influenced by their exposure to so called American dance trends, and by their dance training. Or were they influenced by PHILADANCO's prior repertory? Did they seek to make work that felt that would fit into the company?

Surprisingly, even though they did not see each other's work prior to the premiere performance, there was a distinct commonality in their work. That led me to believe that even though they were given artistic freedom, they were trying to create work that I would approve of. If that was a goal, then they succeeded. But none of the work openly reflected their cultural backgrounds. Thang Dao's ballet was to the music of James Brown. David Brown created a work called *Labess*, after a Tunisian term. Francisco Gella used the music of Philip Glass and Aakash Odedra said that he used dance as his best method of expression, due to his dyslexia. Each never really touched upon their folkloric influences in their work.

This in turn draws my attention to the term *Black dance*. Is it dance done by Black people or music created by Black people, or topics relevant to Black experience? I can never really define the term Black dance or why the term white dance isn't used, because there are white ballets. Those lily-white girls in white costumes; ballets like Giselle and Swan Lake, perhaps that's "white dance". Let us not forget that cultural identity is often disguised by political choices. This can make it difficult to fit into the climate, or decisions are made to fit into the climate and to be accepted by another group. I can easily name many Black artists who openly claim they are not Black, and who are not doing work reflective of their ethnic background. Sometimes they have grown up in a predominantly non-Black community, falling between two worlds and seeking to fit in.

One of Philadelphia's current choreographers, whose work to me has deviated from his previous choreography, now expresses the current environment and angst of the African-American community. It shows his personal experience of history repeating itself, about the police brutality and reflects on some of the acts of violence placed upon Black people during slavery. In his words:

"my work is an exploration of my life experiences, an illuminate assorted cultural legacy which challenges your dancers to impact and touch people."

His early choreography was designed to create beautiful, high energy exciting experiences. That choreographer is Christopher Huggins. Christopher usually comes in and does what we call a "wham bam" ballet. I could always use it to close a show because it was going to be a knock out. This year he choreographed to *Strange Fruit.* He left the people with the question, *"so what are you going to do?"* to make a change about what's happening. It was different for Christopher because he was thinking about what was going on now and not so much of his background.

Another choreographer who grew up in one of the poorer neighbourhoods in Philadelphia studied on one of our programmes at PHILADANCO. He now spends a lot of his time teaching and choreographing in Australia and New Zealand and he also produces a lot of work around classical ballet. This was a surprise to me as his training was not deeply involved in ballet, but I do think that his interest lies in the lack of dancers of colour in the major ballet companies of America. This inspired him to investigate why this was the case. His work aims to enact social radical change for the African-American community and he says his style of work is fuelled by his passion to preserve the Horton technique. But his life experience has shaped the evolution of his work, and the need to make a statement within the work, whilst desiring that the beauty of dance speak for itself.

One of the teachers at my school, who is also staff at the University of the Arts and a choreographer, told me that the broader and more diverse the training and life experiences, the more room the imagination has to create. However, identity can be conscious and personal choice. It can also morph and evolve. Several other chorographers I spoke with could not readily answer how they felt their cultural backgrounds influenced their choreographic vocabularies. They felt that many circumstances around their experiences and training were part of their vocabulary, and not their cultural ancestry. I do suppose that this may have been because I did not explore with practitioners in what Americans call *African dance*.

I have been reflecting upon the words of Kariamu Welsh Asante, an American choreographer who has established an African technique and a curriculum based on dances of Zimbabwe, her comments at an IABD conference several years ago:

"not everyone who ties a cloth around their bodies and plays a drum is truly doing African dance".

In this case it is difficult to disseminate whose work is truly cultural or superficial unless they have studied the many cultures of the continent. Look at what is going on in America. There is a constant reviving of trends. Even now there is a dismissal of serious training. Some true techniques are no longer taught or practiced. Lesser qualified artists are leading the field. The history of Black people in dance is missing from our classes. And the pressure for inclusion in classical ballet continues.

We cannot dismiss what our cultural heritage has given dancers as we continue to create and inform the next generation. The keepers of our history in this field must insist that our contribution is included in the dialogue, or a vast cultural legacy will be lost. Even though we must create new work, we must also archive and preserve our past work. It is a precious treasure, dance is so important to our everyday life. To quote Douglas Sonntag, former director of the National Endowment for the Arts Dance Programme:

"There is something so sublime to a great dancer's performance , it is a language that when well-spoken is incredibly eloquent."

BALLET: THE STRUGGLE FOR VISIBILITY

BLACK DANCERS DID COME UP

DELIA BARKER

I am the former co-director of the English National Ballet School, which is one of the UK's foremost training institutions. It is the official school of English National Ballet Company and provides full time training for students from 16 to 19 years of age. The English National Ballet School has a success rate of 95% on average, in terms of graduates who go on to enter into the ballet industry. In 2018 the school celebrates its thirtieth anniversary.

I must stress that the views of this paper are not the views of the English National Ballet School but my views. I trained as a dancer but I have never been a ballet dancer or a professional dancer. What I can give you is the perspective of being in the Ballet environment for seven years, and my thoughts on the struggle for visibility Black dancers face within the world of ballet.

When I set out to prepare for this paper I did a search on my preferred search engine for Black ballet dancers. Black dancers did come up. So, I thought let me see how visible they are, what does visibility look like? They are there. You get lists of the best female dancers, list of the best male dancers and you get articles. I found it actually wasn't difficult to find Black ballet dancers in 2017. They are doing their own thing, they are there, and they are forging ahead with their careers. But this is very different from the experience I had when I started to dance.

When I was looking for inspiration, I was inspired by stuff that was on TV, videos and a memory of Ipi Tombi. These are the things that I had to look at as a young Black dancer wanting to dance, and it wasn't just Black dancers that inspired me, it was dancers in general. Paula Abdul was my idol because she was a great dancer. It was not until I was about 14 or 15 years old that I came across Phoenix Dance in its original form. Around the same time, a dance teacher took me to see a dance show. I ended up at the London Coliseum seeing Dance Theatre of Harlem. I had never heard of them before but I had the chance to see the *Creole Giselle*. Their work inspired me to make a career out of dancing, and showed that there was an opportunity. I think this was the first time that I saw a possibility of something that I could aspire to. I think that's very different now. Visibility is no longer an issue, you can search for something on the internet and in twenty seconds it appears. So, the issue is not about visibility, but when we talk about dancers we need to know there is a proliferation of Black ballet dancers there. We don't want to have to count them, or list them.

I wanted to know how we can get more Black ballet dancers coming through the system. What are the barriers that are stopping more Black ballet dancers coming through? At the English National Ballet School, they audition about 300 to 400 students per year, globally. Auditions are open to anyone. Over the seven years I was there that would be around 2,800 dancers. Out of those who audition, each year English National Ballet School takes on about 30 students. Over the seven years we are talking around 210 students. Then we look at people who drop out with injuries, or people that change their mind, say we lost about 30 over that period, so now we are down to 180 students. There is on average a 95% success rate, 170 students made it into the classical ballet profession. I can count the Black dancers on my hands. Of those, only one was female. Why is this? Whilst I was at the English National Ballet School I was asked, subtly and very directly, how we were going to diversify ballet. Is ballet racist? Is that why our dancers are not getting through? I do have an opinion but just to get into the dance profession is an upward battle regardless of your colour or background. There are no free passes in it.

One of the things I always asked students when we were interviewing them was how long they had been dancing for. At 15 years old, they would tell me that they had been dancing since the age of two or three, four at the latest. They have been dancing consistently since that age and were typically dancing 15-18 hours of classical ballet per week, on top of other dance forms, and homework. All to get into a school like English National Ballet School. It is really tough. You are not only asking for the commitment of that young person, but you are also asking for years of commitment and dedication from those who support them. This for me is where culture and identity comes into it. When I was growing up, my peer group, my friends and family, did not go to ballet. We actually didn't go to the theatre either, unless we wanted to and the work was relevant. So, we seem to get into a catch 22 because we need to go to see it, see if it is relevant, be inspired and also to aspire to dance, but we are not going. For me there is a question around how culturally ballet sits with us, and how we decide if it is something that we want to engage in. It's a long game as children start so young, it is not they who decide but the people who they have around them and how they are bringing them to the art form. So, how do we increase the numbers? We need to bring young people to ballet.

There is an issue in the UK where we do not see young Black women coming through ballet. I have had a lot of challenging conversations with people about this. Some people have said that we should lower standards, or we should widen opportunities, or we should just accept them because they are young Black girls. But I think to bring someone into a school just because they are a young girl of colour is storing up trouble for that young girl. Ballet is such an exacting art form and by doing that we are not solving the problem. I have also been told that we should be going around the UK scouting for young girls of colour. But even if we find dancers at four years old, they still have a twelve-year journey to take. How do we change the system here in the UK? How do we widen the opportunities so that young people stay engaged with the art form? This is where some of the challenges come in.

As much as ballet is racist, it is also size-ist. I have seen the most beautiful dancers not get an opportunity because they are the wrong size, they are either too small or too tall, and this is irrespective of their background.

I think to say that ballet is racist is simplifying it a lot, but of course racism in ballet does still exist. I know a young Black dancer who graduated from English National Ballet School and had some unsavoury feedback on twitter after he played the Prince. In 2015 people were saying that it is not right that he played the Prince. There was a whole debate on social media about this 20-year-old dancer saying he should not have the lead part because he is Black and everybody knows that the part is white. I have no doubt that all those successful dancers that I talked about before will have had a similar experience when developing their careers. But I do not think the lack of numbers is just about race, it is more complex.

There are purists that sit around ballet that we cannot get away from. For example, there were people whose heads were literally spinning when Akram Khan choreographed Giselle for English National Ballet. That a South Asian choreographer would dare to recreate Giselle, and that the Spanish artistic director in charge of an English institution would allow this to happen. I heard people say that they thought Tamara Rojo had ruined it. For me, it was one of the most stunning things that I have ever seen. So, there are purists that are not going to like any change, whether you are Black, slight, large, too short or too tall. But luckily, they are not the sole decision makers. Now there are wider influences on an audition panel. One thing I can guarantee you is that if there is a talented dancer who walks through the door, they do not care what colour that package comes in. I think the issue lies with the numbers; with the opportunities that are available across the country to get young dancers of colour into ballet. How to transition from ballet being a hobby to making ballet a career seems to be a leap that we are not making. That in itself is a vicious cycle - if people are not seeing it happen for others they are not going to engage in it. It is the visibility of aspiration.

There is not a magic bullet. We are not going to be able
to go suddenly from the position that we are in now in to
having a plethora of Black dancers in companies overnight.
It is a long game, which will take perhaps 10 to12 years.
You might occasionally come across a dancer that happened
to go into a class at 10 years old and was brilliant. But, I am
not sure what it is that we have to do now to change
it for 10 years' time. This is the third time that I have had
this conversation in my career in dance and I am not sure
if we have done enough to change the situation yet.
We are still here counting how many dancers we have,
talking about visibility within ballet. It is an interesting
conversation to have and I wish I had the answer.

Image Credit: Michaela DePrince performs 'Giselle' with the English National ballet (2017).
Photographer Ian Gavan/Getty Images.

LOOKING THROUGH THE KEYHOLE:
BLACK DANCERS IN BRITISH BALLET AND THE INFLUENCE OF THE DANCE THEATRE OF HARLEM

SANDIE BOURNE

INTRODUCTION

When asked, 'Can you name a Black dancer in British ballet?', most people will either name Royal Ballet dancers such as the Cuban former principal guest artist, Carlos Acosta; the British American soloist, Eric Underwood; or the British Kenyan principal dancer, Francesca Hayward. They might also mention African American, Precious Adams, an artist with English National Ballet. However, when trying to recall the names of Black British dancers in ballet, some people may mention Shevelle Dynott, of English National Ballet, or principal dancer Tyrone Singleton with the Birmingham Royal Ballet. Whilst the representation of Black dancers in British ballet is minimal, a total of five in major ballet companies, historically they have always been present, though apparently not well known by the public or by many dance students.

The Dance Theatre of Harlem has influenced many people worldwide. One of the reasons Arthur Mitchell founded the Dance Theatre of Harlem was to establish a company to counteract the lack of opportunities he had experienced in mainstream ballet. He wanted to create an environment where young Black dancers could have the opportunity to train in ballet and in other styles of dance. Mitchell is a role model and an inspiration globally, especially to dancers from the African diaspora. This status was partly created by the fact that he was the first Black principal dancer to perform with the New York City Ballet Company in 1955, at a time when the USA was still practising racial segregation. Consequently, many dancers from the UK are documented as having trained or worked with the company because of the lack of employment opportunities in British ballet companies. This paper aims to highlight the historic representation and visibility of Black dancers in British ballet, through the influence of the Dance Theatre of Harlem.

THE FIRST BLACK DANCER IN BRITISH BALLET

From the 1940s onwards, some of the first known Black dancers to have trained in British ballet institutions were Jamaicans, Berto Pasuka and Richard Riley – who went on to become founders of Britain's first Black dance company, Les Ballets Nègres, in 1946. They both studied with former Russian ballet dancers. Pasuka trained with Anna Northcote (Severskaya) who danced with Ballets Russes de Monte Carlo, whilst Riley took classes with Serafina Astafievia, a former dancer in Sergei Diaghilev's Ballet Russes (Thorpe, 1989, p.172). Although Pasuka and Riley trained in ballet, their company's repertoire was mainly African Caribbean or modern dance styles.

During the 1950s, Johaar Mosaval, a Muslim and Malaysian South African, fled apartheid to become one of the first dancers of colour to train at the Royal Ballet School in 1951 (Corrigall, 2016, online). A year later, he joined the company, formerly known as the Sadler's Wells Theatre Ballet, and worked his way through the ranks to become a principal dancer in 1956. Dedicating twenty-five years to the company, he retired in 1976 and went back to teach in Cape Town. Bearing in mind the historical events of apartheid that Mosaval had escaped in his home country, his presence in the Royal Ballet company demonstrated an unusual level of integration in a historically 'white' art form. Nevertheless, it would be nine years before the first Black British dancer, Noel Wallace, was employed by a company like the London Festival Ballet (now known as the English National Ballet) in 1985.

Image Credit: Susan Lovelle, Paul Russell, and other performers in a Dance Theatre of Harlem production of *Concerto Barocco*. Choreographed by George Balanchine (circa 1974). Photographer Granger Historical Picture Archive / Alamy.

TRAINED IN THE UK AND WORKING ABROAD

During the 1960s, Black British dancers began to train at performing arts institutions; however, finding employment with mainstream ballet companies proved to be extremely difficult. At the time, there were racial tensions directed at immigrants from ex-British colonies, who were in fact recruited to help rebuild the British economy after the Second World War (Fryer, 1984, p. 381).

One example of an artist who struggled to join ballet companies is Christian Holder, who performed at the age of four in his father's (Boscoe Holder) African Caribbean dance company, the Holder Dance Company. Holder studied ballet at the age of seven and joined the performing arts school Corona Academy (known as Corona Theatre School) at the age of eleven in 1960 (Holder, 2014). He learnt Cecchetti and Legat ballet styles; however, once graduating from college, he found no opportunities in mainstream ballet companies at the time. He won a scholarship to train at the Martha Graham School in 1963 and went to the High School of Performing Arts in New York, where he was spotted and asked to join the Joffrey Ballet company in 1966, becoming a principal dancer for thirteen years. Another example of a former dancer who went abroad was Richard Majewski. He is of British and Black heritage, and trained for three years at the Bush Davies Academy in the late 1960s and 1970s (Majewski, 2014). He joined Bejart Ballet in Switzerland in 1970, performing with the company for seven years. From the 1970s onwards, many Black dancers who wanted to pursue a career in ballet also went to train and work in the Dance Theatre of Harlem.

BLACK BRITISH DANCERS AND THE DANCE THEATRE OF HARLEM

Black ballet dancers in Britain faced a similar scenario to the African American dancers who experienced a lack of employment opportunities in Western ballet companies, mainly due to the colour of their skin. In the 1970s Black dancers began to train in British dance institutions, then left to study and work with Dance Theatre of Harlem due to lack of employment opportunities. Examples of dancers who went abroad were Brenda Garrett-Glassman, who was the first dancer to train at the Royal Ballet upper school from 1971–1973. Early on in her training, the school informed her

that they did not employ Black dancers, therefore she did not pursue a career with the company (Garrett-Glassman, 2010). She auditioned for the Dance Theatre of Harlem and trained and worked with the company from 1973 to 1977 (Garrett-Glassman, 2010).

Another dancer who trained during this period was Carol Straker, who studied at Legat School of Russian Ballet from 1974 to1977, and she was the only Black student who attended at the time. Having aspired for so long to join the Dance Theatre of Harlem whilst training at Legat, after seeing a performance at Sadler's Wells, she went to study with the company in 1980 for a year. Unfortunately, she was not employed due to her high level of technical training and skills, which meant they were not able to mould her into their style. Another reason for her unemployment was because she was a dark skinned dancer, compared to the lighter shades of dancers already in the company (Straker, 2002). Dance scholar Nyama McCarthy-Brown also notes a similar occurrence in her research of a dark skinned ballet dancer, Stephanie Powell, who experienced colourism during her time with the company from 1996 to 1998:

'DTH [Dance Theatre of Harlem], for her, was a racially tense environment that exhibited colourism. When asked about the racial tension she experienced, Powell said, 'I never felt so happy to be in a room with fifty African-American dancers and so miserable about the animosity at the same time. [...] On one hand, Stephanie Powell experienced pride in being a member of the longest existing African American company in the world: on the other hand, the divisions within the company lines of color were painful.'

(McCarthy-Brown, 2010, p. 399)

Colourism is an element of discrimination that Black dancers often experience when artistic directors consider them for character roles in narrative mainstream ballets. For example, in the Royal Ballet, Acosta performed more character prince roles in narrative traditional ballets, whilst Underwood danced more modern ballets with the company (Paluch, 2014).

Another dancer who trained during the 1970s is Julie Felix. She trained at Rambert School Ballet and Contemporary Dance from 1974 to 1977. Whilst training, she was nominated by the director of the school, Angela Ellis, to go and work with the London Festival Ballet, where she performed in Rudolf Nureyev's Gala performance of Sleeping Beauty (Plimmer, 2015, p. 74). Felix almost received a contract based on her artistic talents; however, the then director Beryl Grey had concerns about a Black dancer disrupting the aesthetic line in a corps de ballet (Felix, 2015). Felix auditioned for Mitchell in 1976 whilst he was on tour in Britain and she was offered a contract with the company, where she devoted the next eleven years before returning home in 1987. There was clearly an absence of prospective employment in mainstream British ballet companies for Black dancers who wanted to pursue a career in ballet, be able to work in an environment where they felt welcome and to have the opportunity to perform more diverse roles. The migration of Black British dancers to the Dance Theatre of Harlem was noted in the 1976 Community Relations Commission report *The Arts Britain Ignores: The Arts of Ethnic Minorities in Britain* by policy advisor Naseem Khan (1976, p. 105).

Following the 1981 race riots in Britain's major cities (including London, Birmingham, Manchester, Sheffield, Leeds and Liverpool) amongst African, Caribbean and Asian communities in reaction to racial discrimination in employment, education and housing (Fryer, 1984, p. 395), the government commissioned a report to investigate how these issues could be resolved. Judge and barrister Lord Scarman was requested to make this inquiry, the Scarman Report, which *"highlighted the cultural marginalisation of the UK's ethnic minorities, forced a review of funding and cultural policies towards black arts practitioners in the public sphere"* (Donnell, 2001, p. 115). In 1982, projects for ethnic arts and other minority groups would receive funding from the Arts Council and the Greater London Council (GLC) led by Ken Livingstone. An alternate aim for this funding was that minority communities would increase their representation within British arts forms, and therefore increase Labour party votes for the general elections scheduled for June 1983 (Hewison, 1995, p. 238). One of the programmes funded was the Greater London Council Scholarship programme, where grants were given to Black dancers to study with the Dance Theatre of Harlem in the USA; hence the Dance Theatre of Harlem in effect received money from the Greater London Council to train Black dancers from Britain (Akinleye, 2015).

In the 1980s the next upsurge of Black British dancers who trained and went to work with the Dance Theatre of Harlem included Rachel Sekyi, Paul Bailey, Samantha Webb, Adesola Akinleye, Adam and Gregory James (Akinleye, 2015), and Mark Elie (2011), amongst others who went abroad. This resulted in a drain of talent from Britain, showing the ballet establishment that there was a serious lack of opportunity for Black dancers and an absence of integration and diversity in British ballet. During this decade, a change in British ballet began to reverse this, as major ballet companies like London Festival Ballet employed their first Black dancers – Noel Wallace in 1985 and Brenda Edwards in 1987 – whilst Darren Panton became the first Black dancer to graduate from the Royal Ballet School in 1989 (Panton, 2006). The shortage of Black dancers in British ballet during the 1980s was also noted by Graham Devlin, who wrote a report for the Arts Council in 1989 recommending that mainstream ballet schools needed to encourage more Black dancers to join them, and following Devlin's report, things began to change during the 1990s (Devlin, 1989:64).

DANCE THEATRE OF HARLEM AND INTEGRATION IN BRITISH BALLET

During the 1980s and 1990s some progress was made in terms of employing Black dancers in ballet. For example, Evan Williams was the first Black dancer to "be accepted by the Birmingham Royal Ballet's corps de ballet in 1991" (Barrowclough 1991:25). His desire to become a ballet dancer was inspired by watching the Dance Theatre of Harlem on stage as a child. It could be considered that the Dance Theatre of Harlem was the spark that ignited integration in British ballet; for example, in October 1991, the Royal Ballet embarked on a new educational outreach programme called 'Chance to Dance'. This programme provided opportunities for talented children from diverse backgrounds to participate in free ballet classes across the London boroughs of Lambeth, Southwark, Hammersmith and Fulham. The concept was inspired by the then-education officer for the Royal Ballet and the Royal Opera House, Darryl Jaffray, and the director of education for the Royal Ballet, Jane Hackett. The aim of the project was to encourage equal opportunities in ballet for young children within London communities.

The Chance to Dance scheme was inspired by the Dance Theatre of Harlem's outreach programme, which Jaffray and Hackett observed whilst researching outreach dance projects in America (Jaffray, 2010). The project needed to attract dancers from ethnic minorities and therefore Black role models in the field of ballet were required. Although positions with the programme were advertised, at the time there were not enough Black dancers highly trained in British ballet that could teach, so they recruited dancers from the Dance Theatre of Harlem to work on the scheme (Jaffray, 2010). Fortunately, they had a pool of African American classically trained dancers who were already role models and who could assist with the development of the Royal Ballet's project. As part of the agreement, there would be an exchange of Dance Theatre of Harlem's dancers performing roles with the Royal Ballet company. In December 1990, principal dancers Christina Johnson and Ronald Perry performed in the Royal Ballet's Nutcracker at the Royal Opera House in December 1990. Media reports included The Guardian with the headline: "Black swan in to centre stage". Two Black "dancers are to disturb the Royal Ballet's thin, white uniformity", reports Julia Pascal (1990, p. 8). Whilst The New York Times article headlines "Blacks Dance With the Royal Ballet". "London, December 28- For the first time in more than 15 years, the Royal Ballet staged two performances at Covent Garden over the last week that did not have all-white casts" (Cassidy, 1990, online). Although the presence of Black dancers, hence, racial integration was a historic event for the Royal Ballet company in both articles, nevertheless, they did not mention that the performance was part of the Chance to Dance programme. In April 1991, artistic directors Arthur Mitchell and Anthony Dowell signed a two-year agreement to "help diversify the London troupe [...] modelled on DTH's [Dance Theatre of Harlem's] outreach program Arts Exposure" (Dance Theatre of Harlem, 2016 online).

The financial strain of funding dancers from the Dance Theatre of Harlem for the Royal Ballet's Chance to Dance programme meant that this collaboration eventually ended; yet the need for Black dance role models in Britain was still pressing. However, Brenda Garrett-Glassman, Michael Moor, Darren Panton, Patrick Lewis, Evan Williams, and Malachi Spalding, amongst others, would embody the roles of former Dance Theatre of Harlem dancers, and taught and mentored on the programme, becoming true representatives and role models of Black British ballet dancers (Jaffray, 2010).

The founding of the Chance to Dance programme enabled many children from diverse cultures to experience ballet for the first time in London boroughs. Some students even went on to continue professional vocational training in ballet or performing arts institutions throughout Britain. An example of a successful ballet dancer who went on this journey was Shevelle Dynott, who grew up in Brixton and trained through the Chance to Dance programme from the age of seven. In 1997, he was the first Black dancer from the scheme to gain a scholarship to train at the Royal Ballet School (Dynott, 2010). Although he was unsuccessful in obtaining employment with the Royal Ballet Company, Dynott has been employed with the English National Ballet as 'an artist of the company' since 2005.

INSPIRING BALLET BLACK

The Dance Theatre of Harlem inspired Cassa Pancho to found her company Ballet Black in 2001, to generate additional openings for Black and Asian dancers.

The company's mission states:

Ballet Black is a professional ballet company for international dancers of black and Asian descent. We aim to bring ballet to a more culturally diverse audience by celebrating black and Asian dancers in ballet. We perform and offer community driven classes for dancers and students, young and old. Our ultimate goal is to see a fundamental change in the number of black and Asian dancers in mainstream ballet companies, making Ballet Black wonderfully unnecessary.

(Ballet Black, 2016 online)

In 2003 Ballet Black met with former Royal Ballet principal dancer Debra Bull, the former Creative Director for Royal Opera House 2 (ROH2). Bull offered the company rehearsal, training and performance space at the Royal Opera House, Covent Garden, where the Royal Ballet Company were also based (Ballet Black, 2016 online). Journalist and Arts Editor David Lister (2014, online) expressed concerns about the very idea of Ballet Black, a company established because of the lack of opportunities for Black and Asian dancers and based in the same building (at the time) as the Royal Ballet Company– in one of the major mainstream companies these dancers should be performing with.

Image Credit: Arthur Mitchell in George Balanchine's "Agon" (1957) with the New York City Ballet. Photographer Martha Swope. Reproduced with permission of New York Public Library

He states:

They are good, so good that I want to pay them the ultimate and richly deserved accolade – they should be abolished. For I have to pinch myself when I see the Royal Opera House is hosting several nights devoted to a company purely for artists from certain ethnic minorities. Why? If companies such as the Royal Ballet, which is in the same building, are not recruiting sufficient black or Asian dancers, and [are] ignoring their talent, then we need to know about it.

The solution is to hold those national companies to account, not to go off and form a separate and separatist outfit, however brilliant. The arts have to be totally inclusive, or they are worthless. [...] If there is evidence that the big companies really are not recruiting talented Black and Asian dancers, then it is imperative that we are given the evidence, and that the heads of these mainstream, and indeed national, companies are forced to explain themselves in public. The danger is that Ballet Black, understandably delighted with public and critical reaction, will strive less to make themselves unnecessary.

It's a temptation that has to be resisted, because the existence of companies such as Ballet Black perpetuate a belief that we can categorise the arts by skin colour. That is as shocking as it sounds, yet what is Ballet Black doing if not exactly that?

That people can wander past the Royal Opera House in 2014 and say, "Oh look, there's a performance tonight by a company just for black people" is depressing. The dancers and choreographers of the acclaimed Ballet Black should be in the Royal Ballet, English National Ballet, Northern Ballet and the many other dance companies in the UK, classical and contemporary. Ballet Black makes no more sense to me than Opera Black or Film Black or Stand-up Black. In virtually every art form there have historically been difficulties for black and Asian artists in entering the mainstream. And it has been shameful. But, as the gradual success of colour-blind casting in mainstream theatre demonstrates, these difficulties can be addressed, not by forming distinct ethnic minority outfits, but by publicly challenging and even shaming the mainstream into recognising that talent has no ethnic boundaries. Cultural separatism, surely, has to be a thing of the past.
(Lister, 2014 online)

Although, Lister notes that 'cultural separatism' maybe long-gone, in the past it has motivated the establishment of Dance Theatre of Harlem, as dance scholar Christy Adair (1992, p.170) discussed: *"certainly, having a Black separatist ballet company has meant that black dancers have had the opportunity to perform and a good deal of prejudice has been challenged in the process"*. This ideology had influenced Pancho's founding of Ballet Black in 2001, as Lister's piece highlights the fact that Ballet Black represents itself as a separate and or alternative ballet company because of the lack of employment opportunities for Black dancers to mainstream British companies.

Ballet Black currently performs at the Barbican Theatre, whilst the Linbury Studio Theatre at the Royal Opera House is being refurbished. It employs eight dancers, and one is Black British: Jacob Wye, Senior Artist, who also trained on the Chance to Dance scheme and went on to the Royal Ballet School (Ballet Black, 2017). Pancho explained the challenges of finding Black dancers for her company in an interview with journalist Hannah Pool:

In the early days, due to the lack of classically trained Black ballet dancers in the UK, the company took dancers with a more contemporary background, which left them open to criticism. "We weren't able to hold ourselves to the standard of companies like the Royal Ballet," Pancho says, "so people probably made comments about the level of technique. And we didn't always go for a stick-thin look, so I'm sure that's been mentioned."

(Pool, 2010 online)

In 2017, Ballet Black's employment of one Black British dancer is still a reflection of the lack of talent represented or entering the ballet profession in the UK. Pancho's company has enabled students from the Africa diaspora in Britain to train and work in an environment where they can perform diverse roles and colour is not an issue. If Ballet Black was founded at the same time as the Dance Theatre of Harlem, maybe Black British dancers from the 1970s, 1980s would not have had to migrate to America.

CONCLUSION

This paper gives an account of Black dancers in British ballet dating from the 1940s onwards. Although the early dancers were not Black British, dancers like Jamaicans Berto Pasuka, Richard Riley and Malaysian–South African, Johaar Mosaval, trained at the highest level in classical ballet. The racial climate of the 1960s hindered dancers like Christian Holder and Richard Majewski finding employment with mainstream ballet companies and therefore went abroad. During the 1970s and 1980s many dancers would train with mainstream ballet institutions and were hindered by racial discrimination in Britain. Due to the lack of opportunities in mainstream ballet companies, the establishment of Arthur Mitchell and co-founder Karel Shook's Dance Theatre of Harlem in 1969, enabled dancers from the African diaspora to aspire to work with the company and perform many roles. Although, racism stalled Black dancers from entering a career in mainstream ballet companies, 'colourism' in the Dance Theatre of Harlem was found when selecting dancers for employment or when choosing them for roles in repertoire.

The Dance Theatre of Harlem has inspired integration in British ballet, as demonstrated in the example of the Royal Ballet Company's performance of The Nutcracker in December 1990 with African American's Christina Johnson and Ronald Perry, which was part of the agreement of the outreach 'Chance to Dance' programme. This partnership may have empowered both companies, but the lack of Black dancers represented in British ballet was illustrated in important reports written by Naseem Khan (1976) and Graham Devlin (1989) who suggested that changes for opportunities in mainstream training establishments should occur. Since prospects of employment for Black dancers in British companies were minimal, like the Dance Theatre of Harlem, Ballet Black became an institution that provided an opportunity for Black British dancers to find employment. The question still arises, what is the future for Black British dancers' visibility in ballet? Striving for inclusion within mainstream ballet companies or to establish more 'separatist' companies?

REFERENCES

Adair, C. (1992) *Women and Dance: Sylphs and Sirens*. London: Macmillan

Ballet Black 'Mission Statement' Available at: http://balletblack.co.uk/#. (Accessed: 13 July 2016).

Barrowclough, A. (1991) 'Making a splash in Swan Lake', *Daily Mail*. 4 July p.25.

Corrigall, M. (2016) 'A merry dance through gender, religious and racial barriers' *Sunday Times, South Africa*. 23 October. Available at: https://www.pressreader.com/south-africa/sunday-times/20161023/281947427387098 (Accessed: 08/04/17).

Cassidy, S. (1990) 'Blacks Dance with the Royal Ballet.' Special to The New York Times, 29 December. Available at: http://www.nytimes.com/1990/12/29/arts/blacks-dance-with-the-royal-ballet.html. (Accessed: 04/08/15).

Dance Theatre of Harlem (2010) 'Facts Timeline'. Available at: http://dancetheatreofharlem2010.businesscatalyst.com/whoweare (Accessed: 23/04/16).

Dance Theatre of Harlem (2014) 'Outreach, Dancing Through Barriers.' Available at: http://www.dancetheatreofharlem.org/outreach/index.html (Accessed: 23/04/16).

Dance Theatre of Harlem (2015) 'Who We Are, Legacy.' Available at: http://www.dancetheatreofharlem.org/legacy (Accessed: 23/0416).

Donnell, A. (2001) *Companion to Contemporary Black British Culture*. London: Routledge.

Fryer, P. (1984) Staying Power: The History of Black People in Britain: Black People in Britain Since 1504. London: Pluto Press.

Hewison, R. (1995) *Culture and Consensus: England, Art and Politics Since 1940*. London: Methuen.

Khan, N. (1976) *The Arts Britain Ignores: The Arts of Ethnic Minorities in Britain*. London: Community Relations Commission.

Lister, D. (2014) 'Ballet Black is a wonderful company. But it's a shame on the arts that it still exists.' *Independent, 7 March*. Available at: http://www.independent.co.uk/voices/comment/ballet-black-is-a-wonderful-company-but-its-a-shame-on-the-arts-that-it-still-exists-9177277.html (Accessed: 07/03/16).

McCarthy-Brown, N. (2012) *Dancing in the Margins: Experiences of African American Ballerinas*. In Journal of African American Studies, Vol. 15. No. 3, New York: Springer.

Pascal, J. (1990) 'Black swan in to centre stage' *The Guardian*, 20 December, p.8.

Pool, H. (2010) 'Black ballet: Pointe break'. The Guardian, 4 December. Available at: http://www.theguardian.com/stage/2010/dec/04/black-ballet-cassa-pancho, *The Guardian*, (Accessed: 07/03/16).

Plimmer, J. (2015) *Brickbats and Tutus*. London: Austin Macauley Publishers.

Thorpe, E. (1989) *Black Dance*. London: Chatto and Windus.

INTERVIEWS

Akinleye, Adesola (2013) Interviewed, 24 September.

Akinleye, Adesola (2015) Interviewed, 19 December.

Dynott, Shevelle (2010) Interviewed, 14 April.

Elie, Mark (2011) Interviewed, 24 April.

Felix, Julie (2015) Interviewed, 24 August.

Garrett-Glassman, Brenda (2010) Interviewed, 25 May.

Holder, Christian (2014) Interviewed, 5 April.

Jaffray, Darryl (2010) Interviewed 14 June.

Majewski, Richard (2014) Interviewed, 23 February.

Paluch, Matthew Interviewed 22 February 2014.

Panton, Darren (2006) Interviewed, 21 November.

Panton, Darren (2008) Interviewed 10 October.

Straker, Carol (2002) Interviewed, 16 July.

Williams, Evan (2010) Interviewed, 7 June.

Image Credit: Captured, performed by Ballet Black dance company. Choreographed by Martin Lawrance (2017). Photographer Leo Mason/Lebrecht.

RE-INSCRIBING AFRICA'S MULTI-DIMENSIONAL AESTHETICS: RECOGNISING THE CRITICAL PLACE OF IMPROVISATION-AS-PERFORMANCE

MOVING, BREATHING AND BEING: A REFLECTION

FRANCIS ANGOL

REFLECTION: AN OVERVIEW

This paper is a brief supposition looking at the critical place of improvisation as performance, focusing on my rich, diverse and complex heritage and how this has influenced my practice, as well as reflecting on who I am, what I do, how I do it and why I do it.

Re-inscribing Africa's multi-dimensional aesthetics; what does this mean? How am I able to relate to and contribute, as a dance artist, working within the field of contemporary dance art, which is rooted in philosophical teachings and practices of dance from the African diaspora. This paper is thus my contribution, a brief reflection that voices my lived experience of moving, breathing and being, of working within African dance, voicing to further inscribe and re-inscribe the legacy of a people's existence through my work.

OFFERING

I move because I have to, I dance because I am; a resonating, pulsating, organic stream of rhythmic energy, motion in spiritual, physical and emotional flow, drawing from the past to voice within the present, so as to influence the future, connecting and articulating presence with existence to allow the self to prevail.

WHO I AM: THE CREATOR WITHIN

I am a choreographer, performer, community dance practitioner, a somatics movement educator and associate tutor in dance at the University of Surrey. I am also the founder and artistic director of Movement Angol Dance. I am one of the few UK based dance artists that produces work under the genre definition of contemporary African dance. In addition to running my own company I also hold the position of director of dance at Islington Arts Factory, North London's creative hub for art, music and dance.

My former role was that of assistant artistic director and choreographer for Badejo Arts, Britain's former ground-breaking contemporary African dance company, under the directorship of Peter Badejo, OBE.

I am a passionate advocate of the arts, who has been working, practicing the art of physical expression for over 28 years. Over the span of my career, my work has contributed to the enrichment of British dance culture through the production of a range of training programmes, classes and courses and performance works. I work extensively within education, nurturing individuals within professional and community practice, further and higher education and special needs education. I have further contributed to the enrichment of British dance culture by holding the position of trustee on various boards such as Dance UK (now known as One Dance UK), Jacksons Lane Theatre and the previous London Arts Board (LAB).

I am a former fellowship artist of the Arts Council England and graduate of the University of Central Lancashire, with an MA in Dance, Somatics Health and Wellbeing. I have previously held the position of artist in residence at the Jamaican School of Dance, faculty of the University of the West Indies, at the National Dance Company of Nigeria and several UK based dance agencies.

WHAT I DO: THE ENABLER - STIMULATING MIND AND BODY THROUGH EMBODIED CREATIVITY

I deliver creative and engaging dance projects for young people and adult audiences of all ages. Through my work I enable people by creating opportunities for intercultural exchange and dialogue by synthesising cultural traditions with contemporary norms to offer individuals a space for self-actualisation, through expression and exploration. I strive to encourage change by influencing the future through impacting the present with work that is accessible and inclusive.

My work draws from the rich philosophical cultural teachings and dance practices of Africa, influenced by Western dance practices, blended with my Caribbean creole sensibilities, to originate a movement modality I define as contemporary African dance - a distinct language of expression that utilises African dance forms, as the basis for movement development and artistic expression. The approach taken to the work is deeply rooted in the spirituality of the self, a way of life that taps into the unspoken rhythmic dialogue of mind and body, to form a unique cultural synthesis in movement form.

This is especially actualised through my therapeutic bodywork practice BodyRhythms, a therapeutic movement modality that draws from the embodied properties of African dance, offering individuals a fresh and creative approach to engage with their body, to awaken the inner self, through a dialogue of movement, rhythm, dance, imagery and the imagination. The practice is a way of allowing the individual to journey through a widening field of possibilities, folding presence with existence, to allow the self to prevail.

As a performer, choreographer and creative educator, I work to synthesise my accumulated knowledge of dance and the arts with that of my lived experience, to help individuals bring about clarity, meaning and understanding to their lives.

Through movement and dance, I work to help individuals unlock the many possibilities for self-actualisation, growth and development, working to offer people a life enhancing opportunity to bring about a more conscious and connected awareness of oneself, offering creative opportunities to explore personal pathways into the physical and mental body, to reclaim a sense of wholeness from within.

HOW I DO IT: UNFOLDING PRESENCE WITH EXISTENCE

What I do is very much an expression of who and what I am, an individual that has always had a fascination for movement, unchained movement, conscious and unconscious movement, originating deep from within the belly of one's consciousness. Movement for me is the ultimate language of expression, a language that holds no protocols, no grammatical checks or balances, just pure organic articulation, movement in physical and spiritual flow.

In African culture, movement and dance is a fundamental form of communication, a way of life, a people's existence in physical and rhythmic flow. Asante (1996) writes that African movement and dance is context determined.

Within my work, I draw from many African dance cultural practices, and as such improvisation has become a major aspect of my artistic expression and approach. Tierou (1989) writes, Africans tend to be uninterested in any art which lacks improvisation, sculptors, singers, poets, dancers, all are conscious of this fact.

During my training in traditional African dance this was very evident, a practice which was very much part and parcel of the training, especially when working with percussionists. For when working with live music, it was very much about the improvised banter that takes place between musician and dancer, something I had the pleasure of experiencing and learning from during my training. Working in this fashion, to some extent allowed me to be more generous in my creativity, giving myself the space and permission to take risks, through the process of exploration and reflection — to give new meaning to my dance, keeping tradition alive.

I felt that moving from a place not knowing what rhythm or beat that I was supposed to follow or respond to, allowed me to become more aware of my own presence in relation to my body, the space and feelings, rather than thinking how I wanted to move. On hearing the musician's rhythmic poetry through listening by feeling their rhythm, the experience showered my consciousness, connecting me with the moment, stimulating my consciousness to move and be moved.

Improvisation in my work is about moving and creating within a set framework that is rooted within the structural properties of form. This is an approach that creatively allows me to move and express my body in an improvised manner, but being rooted in what I refer to the cultural properties of form.

Tierou (1989) continues to write that:

"Improvisation in African (dance) is not a result, as in the West, of spontaneity but much more of the creative imagination of the improviser who applies themselves to a given subject known to the body".

This for me is very much about the embodied presence - bringing oneself to a place of being that enables one to enter a state of open dialogue with oneself.

THE ROLE OF MUSIC TO IMPROVISING

Working with rhythm, Blom and Chaplin (1988, p. 19) state that:

"All movement contains innate rhythms and phrases which provide the magic ingredient in any of the performing arts."

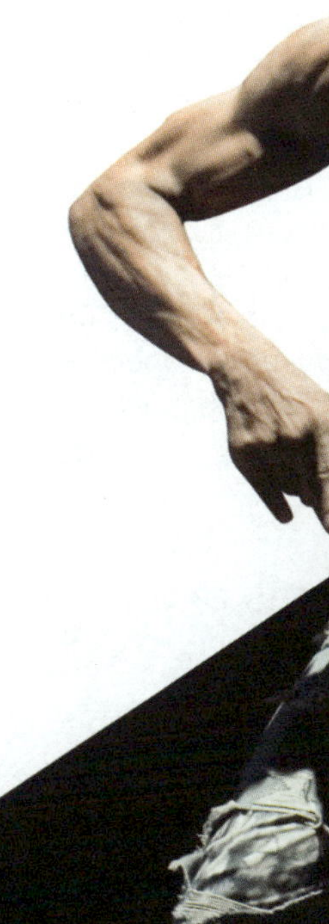

Within the context of improvisation, for me the role of music is of the upmost importance and is a crucial component in the whole process. In my work music does not necessarily dictate my every move but acts as a stimulus, an auditory awakening that resonates through one's consciousness, inviting the body into play, by allowing the conscious self to move into conversation. A polite social interaction between mind and body, to negotiate an outcome, in creating movement that is authentic and seated within the consciousness of oneself.

The role of music and dance are tightly joined and play an important role in African culture and that of the expanding diaspora. Coming from an African or African Caribbean dance background, the engagement with, understanding of, and connection to rhythm is a fundamental part of the training, especially if you are working within the traditional context and working with live music. Music plays a very important part in African life, it helps to bring people together, and acts as a form of spiritual connection to a higher plane, from my perspective, music is like a vine, which weaves and connects during the improvisation process.

Ajayi (1998, p. 20), in her book Yoruba Dance states:

"Through rhythm the ... elements of dance are bound in a harmonious structure".

She continues to say that:

"without rhythm, dance will be no more than a series of disjointed unrelated poses and it will no longer be art."

Although this view may not be shared by all within other dance cultures, for me this clearly affirms the importance and place of music within African life and dance culture.

So, overall, the role of music for me within the improvisation process is such that music acts to expand the imagination, creating a kind of focus group within the consciousness, not directing but unlocking the body, creating avenues for reflection, taking mind and body into an embodied state of being, where one becomes more open and creative to the way one's body senses and feels to move.

WHAT AN IMPROVISER MUST BE ABLE TO ACCOMPLISH WHILST IMPROVISING

During the improvising process a mover should be able to first and foremost aim to establish a state of being that creates a connection between the conscious and the unconscious body, working to develop not a battle, but a conversation, a polite social interaction between the mental and physical body, and in doing so, is able to move into a state of embodiment where one can become more aware of one's presence in relation to one's internal and external environment, giving rise to a state of being where the mover becomes more aware of emotion, allowing them to move from sensation, impulse and feeling to express a more authentic and individualistic way of becoming - because ultimately movement and dance within the performance context for me, is simply an exaggerated expression of one's consciousness .

This sentiment is neatly expressed by Alphonse Tierou (1989, p. 11) when he states that African dance,

"...expresses the most profound experiences of human beings... and is a complete and self-sufficient language" he continues "It is the expression of life and of its permanent emotions - joy, sadness, hope - and without emotion there is no African dance."

DIFFICULTY IN IMPROVISING

Improvising is what we as human beings do every day, so if a dancer has problems improvising, what that may indicate to me is an inability to let-go, an inability to remove one's self from the bedlam of resonating fear and the self-imposed judgement of emptiness, an inability to simply turn off or turn down the noise within one's head and simply allow one's mind and body to exhale, and enter a space where one is able to feel what is happening to the body, when it is happening as it is happening.

Blom and Chaplin (1988, p. 28) state that:

"to improvise is to participate in the creative processes and bring form to the impulses of the body and spirit".

This statement very much underpins my approach to improvisation, which is a major aspect of the process when creating work.

From the position of dance artist, performer and choreographer, movement is the essence of my being. Through movement I am able to learn about and explore myself and my environment. This supports my constant learning of everything I do and of what I am. Even when we think we are not moving, our body is still moving, continuously improvising the dance of survival, within the universe under our skins, moving to maintain our body's natural bounce and flow.

It is only by becoming more aware of ourselves, that we can open dialogue with our body, to allow us through the imagination, to creatively invite our self to initiate an open dialogue with our feelings, emotions and sensations to simply give our self-permission to let go and move with the consciousness to move, and the unconsciousness to be moved.

WHY I DO IT?

I do what I do because:

- It enriches my spirit
- I need to enable others and move people's lives through rhythm and dance
- Dance, and in particular African dance, allows me to have access to places within my consciousness that neither I nor anyone else has access to
- The need to influence change

In summary, as a choreographer, I work with African dance in a very distinct manner. The work not just focuses on engaging with shape and form but uses various elements and devices to allow the dancer to understand the nature of embodied dance; moving from feeling, sensation, emotion and impulse, fundamental principles of African dance culture.

The work and approach to choreography and movement is developed through improvisation and underpinned by somatics practice - an embodied therapeutic movement modality that works to raise the awareness of the individual, so as to allow one to engage more freely with the physical and mental body in a more fluid and intuitive manner. The approach takes the individual on an experiential journey of exploration to allow self-discovery through risk, to unfold.

Rhythm plays another fundamental part of the technique and approach, by working to allow the individual to engage in a discourse that heightens one's awareness to sensation, feeling and emotion, allowing the physical body to play in an improvised banter of mind and body.

In my experience as a dance artist, I find that working in an improvised manner brings a more fluid understanding to the complex polyrhythmic movement dynamics involved in the work.

As a choreographer and performer, I strive to further extend the physicality of the conscious body through my work, moving forward to keeping alive the legacy of a people's existence through what I do, how I do it and why I do it.

REFERENCES

Asante, K.W. (1996) *African Dance: An Artistic, Historical, and Philosophical Inquiry*. Trenton, N.J.: Africa World Press

Tierou, A. (1989) *Doople: The Eternal Law of African Dance*. Routledge

Blom, L. A. and Chaplin, L. T. (1988) *The Movement of Movement: Dance Improvisation*. University of Pittsburgh Press

Ajayi, O. S. (1998), *Yoruba Dance: The Semiotics of Movement and Yoruba body attitude in a Nigerian Culture*. Africa World Press

EMBODIOLOGY® NEO-AFRICAN KNOWLEDGE PRODUCTION

SHERON WRAY

INTRODUCTION

More interesting is what makes intellectual domination possible; how knowledge is transformed from invasion and conquest to revelation and choice; what ignites and informs the [artistic] imagination, and what forces help establish the parameters of criticism.

(Morrison, 1992, p. 8)

Toni Morrison's essay, *Playing in the Dark: Whiteness and the Literary Imagination*, gives voice to my encounter with the substitutions, silences and slippages that foreclose African aesthetics. By this I mean there exists commonly held misperceptions that African people's dance forms are simple folk and vernacular practices, lacking rigour and conceptual underpinning. My enquiries, however, have revealed that which is to the contrary, and it is for those who have eyes to hear, with ears to see, and a willingness to reflect upon the hierarchical manner in which our senses have been diverged away from cognising the philosophical underpinnings of African peoples' knowledges, that such aesthetics becomes abundantly clear.

My approach to art as alliance building is reflected within my ongoing enquiry into improvisation-as-performance, bringing together the fields of dance, music, performance studies, ethnography and cognition. I write from experiential, theoretical and practical knowledge and define myself as a performance architect. This interweaving of thought has led to the revelation of Embodiology®, a neo-African performance strategy, which reflects a hybridity informed by crossing of national boundaries, aesthetic forms and their societal functions[1]. Arguably, disrupting normative disciplinary restraints, separating dance from music, is still considered a necessary part of maintaining an intellectual space for dance studies. However, I would argue that this has created the conditions for dances from the African continent and across the diaspora from being seen on their own terms, which is that they are inseparable from their music, even if this musicality emerges from the dancer's own generation of sound through body percussion, song or stomping. There are several other significant, shared features that are evident across the diaspora, but, arguably, none is more apparently underrepresented or taken for granted than music.

In relearning, undoing and modelling Embodiology® it has been necessary to awaken and reorder my sensory system to navigate various types of performance terrain in which improvisation is a critical performance modality; its architecture has been revealed through enquiry modes of collaboration, ethnography, audience-participation, performance, cultural borrowing and translation, teaching, learning and analysis. Now disseminating Embodiology® as African-centred knowledge, I partake in liquefying frozen concepts of an antique Africa. Positioning West African aesthetic processes, or aesthesis, as the nucleus that generates contemporary praxis, furnishes dance practitioners and educators with an opportunity to experience African sources at the leading edge of the intellectual enquiry and new knowledge production.

My "Afropean" (Eding, 2005) upbringing led the course toward Embodiology® which reflects "Neo-African" (Euba, 2003) expressivity; this improvised aesthesis emphasises values that are found in contemporary and long-standing West African practices, but it also evolves in accordance with forms that are traditionally perceived as Euro-American modes of performance. In reality, these traditional Euro-American practices such as modern dance and various somatic practices are also spectacularly informed by African people's diaspora approaches to movement (Jackson, 2001). For hundreds of years, African people on the continent and in the diaspora, have fed into constructing what has over-archingly been recorded, represented and claimed widely and more often solely as innovations generated by those of European descent. This would extend from modern art practices through to its subsequent derivatives in post-modern, contemporary, futurist art and so on. An alternative presence of African and non-African materials is presented and in this case the 'neo' prefix also recognises that there are European aesthetic values that are embodied imprints that I carry as a UK-born and educated artist who resides in the USA, thus inevitably impacting my perceptual apparatus as I explore Africa's aesthetics.

The core of Embodiology ®, my theoretical and practical conceptualisation of how improvisation is generated, is framed from a re-drafting of West African dance-drumming practices, experienced in the field, followed by deploying artistic space to translate discoveries into models of practice to contemporary dancers and musicians that perform in theatrical settings. Embodiology ®, particularises an understanding of West African practices of improvisation by focusing on interrelated sensory and cognitive processes. To improvise is a critical dimension of performing Africa's dances; improvisation practiced within traditional repertory serves as a vehicle for edification, civic engagement and spiritual communion, among others; it is a collaborative communal practice that advances knowledge production and circulation. Performance studies theorist Margaret Drewal explains that, from a Yorùbá perspective:

"improvisation requires a mastery of logic of action and in-body codes...together with the skill to intervene and transform them" *(1991, p. 43).*

Improvisation from this perspective is dependent upon expertise that builds upon recognised knowledge. Embodiology® enables these aforementioned values to come to the fore, conceptualising aesthetic processes, evident across a broad range of performance contexts that are deeply intertwined with music, and adaptively applying them to generate contemporary performance. Concomitantly, Embodiology's model of improvisation can also be used as an analytical schematic to identify generative strategies deployed within African Diaspora performance practices at large. This latter aspect of Embodiology®, however, is not the subject of this essay; rather the focus is introducing its six principles.

MODEL OF EMBODIOLOGY®

Embodiology®, which comprises six components that interweave aesthesis, evident in Ewe and Yorùbá cultures, also reflects similar African diasporan values that are also identifiable within my own dance genealogy[2]. Embodiology® praxis furnishes individuals and groups of performers with the ability to generate and sustain high level improvisation-as-performance. Its six generative components create an autopoietic system, capable of maintaining and recreating itself. The first of the six principles is dynamic rhythm, the meta-structuring component; it impacts all outcomes through its consciously sustained invocation.

The diagram that follows represents the relationships between Embodiology's six components: dynamic rhythm, fractal code and inner sensing and balance, are represented by the outer ellipses, followed by collaborative competition; play and decision making and audience proxemics, represented as the inner zones. The first three are primary (found across all contexts) and the latter three secondary (contexts dependent with intensity variations); collectively these six components make up the tenets of Embodiology®.

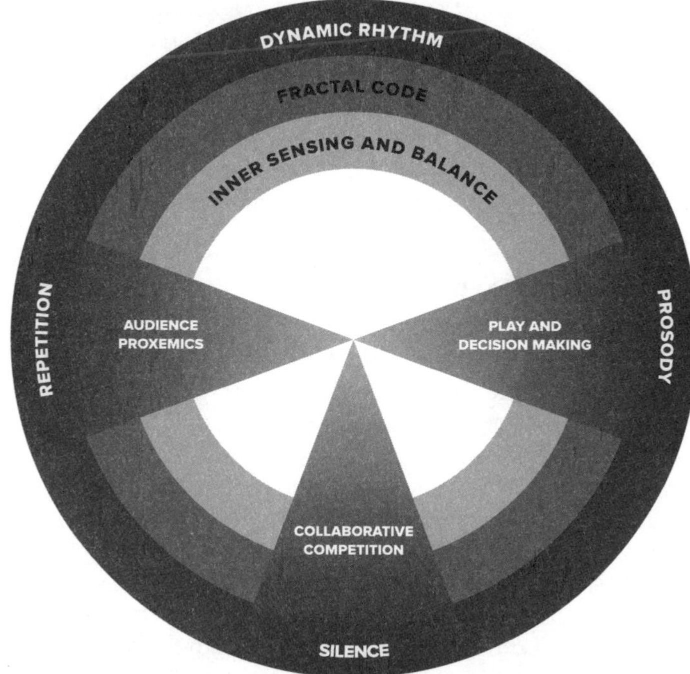

Figure 1. Embodiology® Improvisation Model

DYNAMIC RHYTHM

Dynamic rhythm contains three sub features: repetition, prosody and silence (Nketia, 1992; Welsh-Asante, 1996; Agawu, 1995). It is evident that during performance participants (Ewe, Fanti, Yorùbá, for example) engage in perspicacious listening, identifying and honouring the value of repetition, but not in the mechanical sense, more so as a grounded development of kinaesthetic alliteration (Lyer, 2002). To be responsive, the entire body must be engaged in qualitative listening, to understand how time is musically configured (Stone, 1985). Developing the responsive skill to detect how communication is carried through tone, cadence, duration and pitch is tantamount to informing a sensory-knowing performer, one that can equitably inform the musicians of how they might develop their tonal qualities and inspire further participation. While being able to identify and generate patterns spontaneously, the tacit and sensory values of silence must also accurately be felt.

FRACTAL CODE

Borrowing term 'fractal' from Ron Eglash's examinations of fractals in African design (1999), I apply it in recognition of the importance of repetitious structures that shape social interactions. Each site of performance has a history, custodians, regulated protocols for participation, and an accessible repertory of steps, songs and rhythms, along with a reservoir of memories of past events. Combined, these embody fractal code – a repetitious form, based on known and respected constraints, which manifest at varying scales both temporally and geographically. A performance form can migrate with a people, and while some aspects of the form remain consistent other features are revised in accordance with local, contemporary and cross-cultural currents and tensions. Novelty emerges out of an event's fractal code, its existing repertory projected anew, whereupon continuity is evident. This temporal concept although aurally and kinaesthetically based has similarities to the way an exegesis takes shapes, taking account of the past while creating opportunity for new perspectives to emerge.

INNER SENSING AND BALANCE

The performer's internal somatic landscape has both sensory and cognitive impulses that are capable of generating inspired interventions. Participants' actions evoke emotional connections with others, be they informed audience members or collaborating performers, which dynamically shape the unfolding action. For example, the intentional use of eye contact leads to definite recognition of another participant, a haptic intensification of in-the-moment awareness for both the viewer and the initiator of that connection. This ocular touch triggers sensations that flow into emotion-states, empathy as well as information that promotes total body awareness. Other modes of sensory awareness invoked within Inner Sensing and Balance goes beyond the typical five-sense hierarchical model of perception to include the imagination, kinaesthesia, synaesthesia and intuition; these coalesce to produce layered, often exaggerated impulses that unceasingly stimulate interactions as a performance unfolds. Vitally, the performers' 'intersensory' (Sacks 2003: 233) worlds, as it extends outward, invokes the presence of joy, as an aesthetic value, an enduring concern of Embodiology®.

PLAY AND DECISION MAKING

With the intensity of new information that is present in a performance where improvisation shapes the proceedings, performers make in-the-moment decisions conscious, foregrounding the use of executive brain function (Diamond, 2011). Harnessing these skills, performers demonstrate flexibility, responsivity and resilience within rapidly changing environments. Revealing new ideas out of familiar material is invoked by a commitment to discovery through investigative play. A kindling current is evident in performers as they stay kinaesthetically curious about repertoire (fractal code) which can lead to redrafting of steps in newly imagined ways, further fuelling the performance. Executive brain function foregrounds deductive reasoning, short and long- term memory, making it possible to deploy an extensive range of interventions that may also include ironic play; non-action is such. Courage is displayed through a corporeally reasoned sense of daring, whereby making highly provocative choices are enacted so as to demand that others reflexively respond; and on the part of the audience such involuntary reaction can create lasting effect, well beyond that of the performance.

COLLABORATIVE COMPETITION

Seemingly an oxymoron, this clause represents a type of competition that is found within members of the same team. In such cases an individual's efforts towards excellence propels others within their group to aspire to achieve greater levels of mastery. In this way individuals collectively energise and sustain performance through overtly challenging each other, themselves or even the audience in a series of brinkmanship activities where parody, proximity and outmaneuvering are tactics in common. Through these strategies virtuosity is abundantly displayed. Broadly speaking, in many West African and diaspora contexts we can see that improvisation engenders expert dancers to compete (Jackson, 2001) and, in such cases where status is actually at stake, enigmatic brilliance flows. Such high accomplishment critically demonstrates innovation through rhythmic perspicuity combined with movement invention, all performed according to the constraints of the style of that particular movement practice. In this way demonstrations of musical distinction and movement style create increasing levels of competitiveness that yields a collaborative mode of instantaneous learning and innovation. In these instances, individuals observe each other closely, using skills of mimesis, satire and ironic play (Daniel, 1995; Drewal, 1992). An informed audience's attentiveness to this communicative jousting brings critical attention to co-creators' inventions, resulting in re-inscriptions of their community's values, continuity and identity.

AUDIENCE PROXEMICS

The audience is not assumed to be a fixed entity made of homogeneous observers. Rather, they are well-informed (to varying degrees) and considered potential co-creators of the scalable activity; they may for example only engage on a subtle level, partaking by head nodding or foot tapping, or indeed, on another scale they could simultaneously be the performers, as in a processional performance. The performance space that they occupy is also porous, an entity through which action flow or dissolve; they are often circular to create inclusiveness and promote access. The participants acknowledge the presence of musicians but at any given moment performers may choose intentionally to direct their focus toward a particular section of the audience; by doing so the communicative experience of those observing from that spatial perspective is heightened. The unpredictability and surprise that changing proximal foci brings affects all the other observers since they too, at any moment, could be in direct engagement with a performer whose will to enact sudden proximal change remains unpredictable, albeit it temporary. Alongside this volatility, it is expected that audience members include those who have expert knowledge, and it is they who deem a virtuosic performance worthy of praise or dismissal through their palpable appetites or diminished engagements with the performance as it evolves and this may be demonstrated in a number of ways, from giving praise, participating or giving money to the dancers, singers and musicians.

Having briefly outlined these laws that together generate performance improvisations it must be said that knowing them theoretically is quite some distance away from turning these seeds into a fertile practice.

However, there is still a great need for theoretical knowledge that can help with revealing knowledge of the technologies underpinning African people's practices. With an understanding of these six improvisation-as-performance structures, foregrounding dance and music, they can be harnessed beyond practice to also function as an analytical tool. Recognising the pervasive role that improvisation plays within continental Africa and its diasporic continuum, Embodiology® can be deployed not only to generate contemporary performance but also to analyse and critique many different forms of dance and music.

In almost every dance innovation in the African diaspora - from plantation dances to capoeira, tap dance to the Charleston, jitterbug to breaking, jazz to hip hop - improvisation, freestyle or spontaneity is either at the forefront of the activity or its complete mode of operation. Embodiology®, as analytic theory, allows new, African-centred evaluations to be enacted on such phenomena. Consider the definitions and workings of dynamic rhythm and fractal code alone, these permit entirely new readings on historic, current and future dance and music formations, with critical perspectives of aesthetic values that have been under-examined. Effectively, Embodiology's praxis is an alternative to other movement analysis systems which because of their movement focus have limitations in assessing these dynamically music-natured forms.

REFERENCES

Agawu, V.K. (1995) *African Rhythm : A Northern Ewe Perspective*. New York: Cambridge University Press.

Asante, K.W. (1996) *'The Zimbabwean Dance Aesthetic: Senses, Cannons and Characteristics'* in K.W. Asante (ed.) African Dance: An Artistic, Historical, and Philosophical Inquiry Trenton, N.J.: Africa World Press, pp. 202-220.

Burns, J. (2010) *Rhythmic Archetypes in Instrumental Music from Africa and the Diaspora*, Society for Music Theory, 16 (4), pp. 4-40.

Daniel, Y. (1995) *Rumba: Dance and Social Change in Contemporary Cuba*. Bloomington : Indiana University Press.

DeFrantz, T. (2002) *Dancing Many Drums : Excavations in African American Dance*. Madison, Wis.: University of Wisconsin Press.

Diamond, A. (2013) 'Executive Functions', *Annual Review of Psychology*, 64 (1), pp. 135-168.

Drewal, M.T. (1991) *'The State of Research on Performance in Africa'*, African Studies Review, 34 (3), pp. 1-64.

Drewal, M.T. (1992) *Yoruba Ritual: Performers, Play, Agency*. Indiana University Press.

Eding, J. (2005) '…and I let myself go wherever I want to', *Agenda*, 19 (63), pp. 131-132.

Eglash, R., (1999) *African Fractals: Modern Computing and Indigenous Design*. New Brunswick, N.J. : Rutgers University Press.

Euba, A. (2003) 'Concepts of Neo-African Music as Manifested in the Yoruba Folk Opera' in I.T. Monson (ed.) *The African Diaspora: A Musical Perspective*. New York and London : New York: Routledge, pp. 207-241.

Jackson, J.D. (2001) 'Improvisation in African-American Vernacular Dancing', *Dance Research Journal*, 33 (2, Social and Popular Dance), pp. pp. 40- 53.

Iyer,V. (2002) 'Embodied Mind, Situated Cognition, and Expressive Microtiming in African-American Music', *Music Perception*, 19 (3), pp. 387-414.

Monson, I. (2008) 'Hearing, Seeing, and Perceptual Agency', *Critical Inquiry*, 34 (S2), pp. 36-58.

Morrison, T. (1992) *Playing in The Dark: Whiteness and the Literary Imagination*. Cambridge, Mass.: Harvard University Press.

Nketia, J. H. K. (2002) 'Musicology and Linguistics: Integrating the Phraseology of Text and Tune in the Creative Process', *Black Music Research Journal*, 22 (2), pp. 143-164.

Sacks, O. (2003) 'The Mind's Eye', *New Yorker*, 28, pp. 48-59.

Stone, R. M. (1985) 'In Search of Time in African Music', *Music Theory Spectrum*, 7, pp. 139-148

FOOTNOTES

1. Embodiology® is a registered trademark and as such demonstrates my commitment, as an action researcher, to return a royalty payment to the Ewe community in Ghana each time its principles are shared in full or in part.

2. My multimodal methodology combining strategies from within autoethnography, Practice-as-Research, action and grounded theory.

NUANCED CONTEMPORARY GHANAIAN IDENTITY:

NEGOTIATING NEW CHOREOGRAPHIC BARRIERS AND MULTIFACETED AESTHETICS

TERRY BRIGHT KWEKU OFOSU

Early choreographers in Ghana somewhere in the mid 1960s were students who were trained at the School of Music and Drama, now the School of Performing Arts. These choreographers based their creative philosophy on the idea postulated by Mawere Opoku, the pioneering father of dance and first Artistic Director of the Ghana Dance Ensemble. The 'sankofa' (go back and retrieve from the past) idea is what these dance trainees in Ghana used as their creative philosophical base for several years. Opoku's numerous choreographies with the Ghana Dance Ensemble and those of his trainees such as Ofotsu Adinku and F. Nii Yartey were based on the 'sankofa' philosophy, making them typically Ghanaian.

The Ghanaian social dynamics today presents a different 'space' for creativity. In fact, the cultural and physical spaces have shifted and continue to shift due to new developments, urbanisation and to a large extent globalisation. It is these 'shifts' that are inadvertently affecting and shaping the Ghanaian aesthetics and pushing new boundaries of creativity and establishing new identities.

Today's creative dance environment is characterised by the confluence of traditional dance idioms, new creations (improvisation) and popular dance idioms, all of which are recognised as Ghanaian identities, yet some school of thought believe popular dances are not. As a choreographer who was trained at the School of Performing Arts, University of Ghana, I have to negotiate the creative terrain informed by my: philosophical foundation in choreography, the nuanced Ghanaian psyche and attitude towards dance, the economic demands as well as the politics of creating dance in Ghana.

BACKGROUND

From an academic perspective, choreography in Ghana can be traced back to the establishment of the School of Music and Drama, and the Ghana Dance Ensemble in 1962 as part of the Institute of African Studies (Asiedu, 2014, Adinku, 1994). The establishment of this iconic institution was against the backdrop of Ghana's independence in 1957. Due to the legacy of the colonial interregnum, the nascent Ghanaian nation had to deal with socio-culturally scarred citizens (Nkrumah speech in 19631, as compiled by Obeng, 1997; Nii-Yartey, 2016). Citizens whose existence *lacked a dynamic relation between cultural values and national orientation* what Kwame Gyekye (2013) calls *'evolutionary disconnect'* (xxiii). The formation of the Institute of African Studies, and its concomitant subsidiary arts sections, coincided with Ghana's premier president's Pan Africanist and nationalist movements. The activities of the Institute of African Studies were to serve as an antidote to the colonial legacy (Nii-Yartey, 2016). The creative philosophical orientation of their pioneering students, some of whom later became lecturers, has served over time as the foundational philosophy of the School of Performing Arts, University of Ghana. How can products of the School of Performing Arts, through their created works, deal with audiences who are psychologically and culturally scarred and who vacillate between Africanism and Westernisation in the current global mix? The answer to the above question can be found in Sharon Bell's conclusion of her contribution to the anthology in practice-led research, in the creative arts.

Ghanaian Dancers, South Bank London - Dave Booth/Alamy

She writes:

> "yet more open 'research' paradigms and methodologies are needed to generate understanding of our academic modes of production and a more nuanced understanding of the place of creative production within the academy"
>
> *(2009, p. 261).*

Bell's conclusion advocates for a cautionary approach in analysing and assessing how the creative methods of academics are formulated and how they affect academic modes of production. In Ghana, therefore, the original approach was to research into traditional dance practices, isolate their various movement components and idioms and use them as foundational materials to create new dances. These newly created dances could be in the form of neo-traditional dances or contemporary African dance.

THE PROBLEM

The difficulty here is that today the Ghanaian, still to a large extent, hold on to some of the colonial legacies, especially issues such as language, taste, ideologies, structural organisation of modern institutions (schools, governance) et cetera (Gyekye, 2013, Manuh and Sutherland-Addy, 2013). A quagmire of ideological and identity battles often engages the Ghanaian psyche, especially on issues concerning the contemporary Ghanaian.

Scholars in the arts have also had a fair share of these convoluted ideologies and 'psychological distortions'. For the performing arts scholar, therefore, negotiating this complex psychological terrain is a daunting task. It is against this backdrop of schisms between Eurocentrism, Westernisation and the move for a Ghanaian national identity (by extension Pan Africanism) initiated by Kwame Nkrumah (Adinku 1994, p.6) that Manuh and Sutherland-Addy (2013) write:

> "this becomes even more important when we consider the need for knowledge on Africa that is not Eurocentric or sensationalised, but driven from internal understandings of life and prospects in Africa"
>
> *(p.1).*

The pioneering teachers in the arts adapted this Afrocentric approach to creativity as a way of restoring the 'atypical identity-legacy' bequeathed to the Ghanaian to normalcy.

SOME IMPORTANT QUESTIONS

In my interrogation of this paper's topic, I tend to identify two main 'how' research questions, which allows for the fleshing out of the various components that influence my choreographic practice.

How do the nuanced Ghanaian historical, socio-political, aesthetic and cultural spaces influence choreographic praxis, more especially my approach?

How do I negotiate the new Ghanaian interdisciplinary dance terrain, whilst employing improvisation as performance as a vital point of departure?

The elements that influence my choreographic approaches are myriad and very nuanced. They stem from a cultivated habit over decades of dance practice that spans from my teen days as a street dancer in the 1980s, through my tertiary training at the School of Performing Arts in the 1990s, to my current position as a lecturer and practitioner. To do justice to these questions, I first of all expatiate on how the Ghanaian identity has been shaped over the years, and how that has influenced performing arts scholarship at the University of Ghana, which was the sole performing arts academic institution for decades in the country.

THE GHANAIAN IDENTITY

During the colonial era, all efforts were made through oppression and European racism by the colonial masters (Ajei 2011) to denigrate the vibrant Ghanaian culture through indoctrination, the barrel of the gun and the bible (Saah and Baaku, 2011; Nii-Yartey, 2016). There was a ban on drumming and dancing and even the wearing of traditional clothing in churches (Agordoh, 2002). Four categories of indigenes emerged during the colonial period of the British in the Gold Coast (Ghana): the disgruntled Gold Coast Euro-Africans, who served as economic, political and social intermediaries for the colonial masters - and who were weeded out after the discovery of the causes and cure of malaria; those who whole-heartedly embraced European culture by rejecting theirs, and aspiring to become like the colonial master; those who totally detested the colonial masters and fought them such as the Ashantis and some indigenous intellectuals; and those who lived in the hinterland and were not bothered about what was happening (Saah and Baaku, 2011). The British gained grounds and gradually became a de facto colonial power, very dominant and pervasive. Their influence on a portion of the citizenry was remarkable. Such indigenes saw anything that is beautiful as a product of the white man. The latter assertion is reflected in some Ghanaian languages that prefixes the word 'white person(s)' – blofo (Ga dialect) and in the Akan dialect abrofo (plural) or broni (singular) before the names of fruits such as pineapple, cashew nuts, and even beautiful daughters and sons are sometimes referred to as 'my white person' (me broni). The practice is an indication of the legacy of the colonial master that continually downplayed the African identity as inferior, which is evidenced in their application of tabula rasa to reinvent the indigenes after the European configuration (Asante, 2006).

GHANAIAN CHOREOGRAPHERS IN ACADEMIA

Now, since the School of Music and Drama (later to be named the School of Performing Arts) was the sole institution that trained artists in academia, the Afrocentric philosophical approach in teaching became the status quo. For decades, the school continually churned out students based on this philosophy.

Ofotsu Adinku, one of the pioneer dance students, who was trained by Mawere Opoku and J.H. Nketia, the founding fathers of the Music and Dance programmes, claims in his book:

"Within the Institute of African Studies was the School of Music and Drama whose Research fellows were charged by Government with the responsibility of carrying out research and offering instruction in the traditional performing arts, as well as establishing processes for development of new arts forms based on traditional models."

(p. 1)

Adinku's assertion is an indication of the underlying philosophical orientation of products of the School of Performing Arts, University of Ghana for several years. Of course, new global academic approaches were also fused into the Ghanaian method of teaching dance especially in areas such as composition, Labanotation, dance analysis, et cetera. Yet, to a large extent, teaching methodology in dance, and more importantly choreography, relied on traditional materials:

"In terms of practical activity, the choreographic development of Opoku is significant for dance education. His application of traditional artistic features into new choreographic art would guide students and choreographers seeking methods for applying traditional models in new choreographic developments."

(Adinku, 1994, 3)

In fact, Opoku and Nketia trained the first generation of lecturers such as Ofotsu Adinku, Ampofo Duodu, Patience Kwakwah, F. Nii Yartey and Asare Newman. The first generation transferred this philosophical orientation by training a second group made up of Oh! Nii Sowah and Akua Abloso, who joined the first generation also to groom the third generation. It is this general philosophical orientation that has shaped my choreographic style. However, I am continuously being centrifugally drawn towards the existing global influences that pervade our society, and is what makes me interested in popular dance as a research area, which I will discuss later in the paper.

Today, the hodgepodge Ghanaian creative-scape is as a result of a couple of factors. First of all, the effects of colonialism that made some citizens repudiate Ghanaian cultural practices such as the arts ('Dondology')[2]: Secondly, the effort made by Kwame Nkrumah, to re-cultivate the love for Ghanaian cultural practices, which was mirrored in activities of the School of Performing Arts. Thirdly, the effects of the new paradigms in scholarship, the multiplicity of knowledge and inter-disciplines, shifting 'spaces' and the general global influences through technology and advancement of society, presents a new phase for creativity. The choreographer will have to deal with such challenges randomly, in producing work that will meet the needs of the complex Ghanaian audiences. An audience that looks for authentic Ghanaian cultural practices in one breath and unconsciously rejects it in another breath; a new generation that are so attracted to Western culture, almost invariably losing their language, quotidian cultural practices and identity. The Department of Dance Studies' trained choreographer will approach creativity as presented by Hargoe and Salifu:

'The Department of Dance Studies puts Nkrumah's ideologies in perspective and has sought to make dance responsive to the social needs of society'

(2014, p. 96).

And, what are the social needs of society? Some of these needs I have indirectly mentioned above such as: identity, power, a voice of representation, psychological healing from colonial scars, et cetera. Also important are the challenges of modern Ghana that needs solutions such as poverty, lack of progress and development in areas of economic growth, governance, health, education, gender equality and many more. In choreographing dances to address such challenges, the scholar choreographer will have to rely on 'movement aspects of customary behaviour' and symbolic and other coded messages from the traditional society (Yartey, 2006).

In addition, one quotidian Ghanaian traditional practice, which is often employed by choreographers in academia, is improvisation. In the traditional society, a common practice amongst performers is creating on the spur of the moment or ad libitum. The approach is what I refer to as 'extreme improvisation' (extemporaneous), which opens up created works for surprises. Whilst improvisation in the traditional Ghanaian society is mostly based on the extreme approach executed through solo performances, its application in current choreographies ranges from exploration at the initial stages of choreography, to extempore solo performances. Further discussions on improvisation will be done under the sub-topic 'My philosophy and theoretical approaches.'

Most of the solutions to the discussed issues above in Ghana are chaperoned by government with the support of corporate and non-governmental organisations. Ghanaian choreographers must find ways of providing solutions through creative works custom-made for academia, government, the society at large, corporate bodies and non-governmental organisations (NGOs). The latter considerations have added to my philosophical orientation, especially creating for corporate bodies and NGOs.

MY CHOREOGRAPHIC PHILOSOPHY AND THEORETICAL APPROACHES

From the above discussions, what have really informed my philosophical orientation to choreography in a nutshell, are:

- The social construct that I became cognisant of in my early days as a teen, which is cherishing anything that is foreign, especially that from the Western world

- The pride in my culture as taught by the Department of Dance Studies University of Ghana, especially how to use cultural elements in choreography

- The influences on me as a result of my dancing on the streets as a freestyle or popular dancer, which has caused my affinity to popular approaches in the arts

- My encounter with corporate bodies whose creative demands caused me to experiment severally with choreopoems, a way of blending poetry with dance to project client messages.

What I intend to say in the above outline is iterated in Isidore Okpewho's book African Oral Literature, which suggests that an artist's career is influenced or shaped by his/her environment (1992). Blom and Chaplin (1982, p. 216) corroborate Okpeho's assertion that *"The choreographer's whole life, personality, and education form the matrix from which she creates."* The above outline forms my matrix, which also makes me come across as an eclectic choreographer, but I have always favoured choreographies based on a blend of traditional and popular dances. In fact, my graduate thesis project was based on the concept of synthesising traditional and popular dances (Ofosu 2009). From a choreographic perspective, I theorise dance into four categories, three of which are derived from John Martin's (1965) theories: (1) indigenous, traditional, and ethnic dances, passed on from generations; (2) popular and recreational dances- primarily for edification and amusement (Martin, 1965; Dodd, 2009; Ofosu, 2014; Barber, 1987); (3) pure (Smith-Aurtard, 2000) or spectacular dance (Martins, 1965) and (4) expressional or 'message-driven' dances.

In recent times, however, I have been more engaged with corporate bodies, which often requires for more communicative and self-explanatory dances.

Such engagements have made me rely heavily on choreopoems, which has resulted in a publication on choreopoems, titled Dancing to Words, Ideas and Rhymes (Ofosu and Sowah 2014). All these choreographies are created against the notion that the Ghanaian dance audiences are not as sophisticated as the western ones, and therefore dances should not be too abstract.

Some theoretical perspectives that have shaped my creativity are Gestalt psychology and symbolic interactionism (Waskul and Vannini 2006); their combined influence on my embodied choreographic praxis is strong. Gestalt psychology according to Terry Eagleton (1996) is a branch of psychology that concerns the human mind and perception; the human mind in effect internally formulates a perception about the world. It is concerned with the integration of discrete perceptions into an intelligible whole. Gestalt here means perception. Rudolf Arnheim avers that *'Gestalt psychology did offer the first scientific tools for the structural analysis of wholes'* (1970, p. 85), especially with regards to global figures or the chaotic world, instead of gathering smaller images of unconnected diverse forms (Carlson and Heath, 2010). Embodiment through Gestalt psychology will therefore mean imbibing those perceptions of the world, to reproduce or represent them through activities of the body.

Symbolic interactionism is technically a constellation of core ideas gleaned from American pragmatism:

Pragmatists

"Emphasise human beings as active and creative agents; a human world that both shapes the doings of people and is fashioned by the doings of people; a determined emphasis on how subjectivity, meaning, and consciousness do not exist prior to experience, but are emergent in action and interaction…"

(As cited in Waskul and Vannini 2006, Reynolds 2003: 45–46).

The above quotation is an indication that symbolic interaction is a very nuanced process involving creative bodies, in constant engagement with other bodies and the environment, producing a result that is in itself is processual and very emergent. In my position as an academic and a choreographer, the constellation of ideas that engages with me from the institutions that trained me on one hand, and the society I grew up in on the other hand, become materials that inform my persona. I have therefore built a personal schema that is gleaned from Gestalt psychology (perceptions from society) and symbolic interactionism. These schemas over time have become embodied and therefore are manifested as my choreographic philosophies, which is using traditional dances and Ghanaian and African customary practices as resource material to create new dances. I have also been influenced by the political academic climate, economic exigencies and my life as a freestyle dancer, which have reshaped my choreographic philosophy.

PERSPECTIVES ON IMPROVISATION IN CHOREOGRAPHY

Within my choreographic schema is a choreographic approach, which is vital to the creative arts and the very essence of the practitioner's work, teaching, creation and performance: that is improvisation. Blom and Chaplin define improvisation as:

'the practice of creativity'… 'it serves as a preparation, a mental-physical-emotional "seeding of the bed" from which the choreography will grow'

(1982, p. 5).

Most choreographers often view improvisation as the driving force of creativity, it is employed as a preparatory facet of the choreography, where movements are developed and suitable ones are selected. Nora Ambrosio (2003) observes that choreographers use improvisation as a means of creating new movements, which are then integrated into the dance. She also expatiates on another form of improvisation she refers to as *'creative movement'* that is more open and

accommodating to a fault (2003, 103). In fact, astute dance critic, John Martin (1965) believed that the *"original creative impulse of modern dance"* was based on improvisation. He expresses improvisation as the *"concept of inner vision and invoker of art"* that is derived from *"chance and happenstance"* or serendipity (Anderson 1965). Martin's assertion is linked to my earlier explication on *'extreme improvisation,'* which has to do with performing without any preconceived thoughts on the movements letting one's self go. Jacqueline M. Smith-Autard refers to the latter as free improvisation or *"an open, free spontaneous response in movement"* in *"impromptu, unforeseen ways"* (2000, 81). It is when exploration as described by Smith-Aurtard combines with improvisation that choreography comes to fruition. 'Extreme improvisation' or freestyle dance is one of the important 'philosophical legacies' of the Department of Dance Studies, a direct influence from the traditional dance practices. In almost all traditional dance and music performances, performers are at liberty to improvise especially as solos, and that is a standard practice.

I am a dance practitioner who prior to joining the dance scholarship had won the Ghana National Freestyle Dance Championship in 1989, so I see myself as a freestyler or improviser. I am currently in a PhD programme and my area of interest is popular dance and its rhetorical expressions, which is also linked to improvisation. Popular dance in its expressive form is basically freestyle dance, which is technically produced through improvisation or serendipity. As a scholar I teach composition, choreograph dances every now and then, and I teach popular dance technique. In all these areas in my practice I make good use of improvisation. I do employ improvisation in my choreographies as a way of emphasising or echoing a particular idea, sometimes as a stopgap or interlude. Improvisation in my choreographies also serves as moments of spectacle, and also for highlighting particular characters such as the antagonist or protagonist. It also provides a platform for surprises and may change in every performance. Most often, I introduce improvisation through solo performances of the very adroit dancers, whose experience in performance allows them to move freely without inhibitions.

In teaching composition and/or choreography, the creativity starts by mooting a stimulus and allowing my students to explore and improvise with movements. In some instances, students are led to improvise out of nothing to develop their own themes. One other important form of improvisation, which I use in teaching, is contact improvisation, where dancers have to keep a part of their body in contact with their fellow dancers while dancing. From my experience, students who cannot improvise are those who are coy and less expressive in their verbal communication. With constant practice, however, some coy students have managed to break loose and become eventually dexterous improvisers.

Employing improvisation when I am performing is very dicey, due to the enormity of movement vocabulary I possess as a veteran dancer. I have so much movement stored up in my memory that it is somewhat difficult improvising during performance, because movements automatically pop up, depending on what type of music is being played. Certain music types evoke specific dance movements, which may be stored in my sub-conscious mind, and these dance movements may be performed as improvisation but in actual fact they are not. In my field of practice improvisation is perceived as a prelude in composition or choreography, a tool that the choreographer uses to create their movements and develops them further into the whole piece. Improvisation can serve as catalyst at the beginning of the creative process and also be used during the main performance in the form of free styling. During the main performance, it is mostly experienced dancers, who are chosen to improvise, which suggests a showcasing of skill, spectacle and surprise ('the three s').

CONCLUSION

Creativity is a very processual and rhizomatic activity, it has always been fluid and therefore allow artists to have options and also experience new approaches. Two main areas affect the artist's creative ability: external and internal influences. The external influences the physical (environment) and cultural spaces (identity, religion, ethnicity, et cetera), power contestations, economic and financial constraints and society's aesthetic sensitivities, psyche, knowledge on the arts. The internal influences will include the individual's psyche, knowledge on the arts, affective or visceral experiences, beliefs, philosophical foundation in the arts and intelligence.

In this paper, I have discussed how the colonial masters' activities have scarred the Ghanaian's psyche and aesthetic sensibilities and the repercussions on the creation of a peculiar Ghanaian educational system. I have enunciated on how the philosophical foundations of the School of Performing Arts, University of Ghana, with its interest in traditional values, have influenced my approach to choreography. I have examined how other influences have all helped to shape my choreographic approaches, such as the Ghanaian psyche based on the social construct as a result of colonisation, my experiences as a freestyle or popular dance enthusiast, my choreographing for corporate bodies and NGOs. I have also elucidated my understanding of improvisation as (1) a prelude-creative tool for composition and choreography, and (2) as an applicative material in performance as freestyle, improvisation, serendipity or 'letting oneself go' without a preconceived notion. I have also discussed how and why I have used improvisation in my choreographies, as a solo performance by dexterous dancers, for echoing or emphasising an idea and to showcase dexterity, spectacle or a surprise. The challenges of the scholar/creator and the conditions that shapes his/her philosophy is encapsulated in Sharon Bell's reality statement:

In reality, many colleagues in higher education would say that their creative output is: (1) derivative due to their preoccupation with comparative practice (2) compromised due to the unbounded demands of teaching and conventional research (and now add community engagement and consultancy) (3) technically underdeveloped due to the lack of time and space to refine the realisation of creative concepts (4) highly theorised and therefore less accessible to an audience (5) conservative due to the high levels of accountability and uniformity demanded by the contemporary university. (2009, pp. 252-53)

REFERENCES

Adinku, O. (1994). *African dance education*. Accra: University Press

Ågordoh, A.A. (2002). *Studies in African music* (revised edition). Ho: New Age Publications

Ambrosio, N. (2003). *Learning about dance: Dance as an art form and entertainment.* Iowa: Kendal/Hunt Publishing Company

Anderson, J. (1965). 'Introduction'. In Martin, J. *The dance in theory.* New Jersey: Princeton Book Company Publishers.

Asante, E. (2006). 'The relationship between the chieftaincy institution and Christianity in Ghana.' In Odotei, I. K. and Awedoba A. K. (Eds.), Chieftaincy in Ghana: *Culture, governance and Development* (pp. 231-246). Accra: Sub-Saharan Publishers.

Ajei, O. M. (2011). 'Africa's renaissance and the challenge of culture: The failures of NEPAD'. In Lauer, H. Amfo, N. A. A., and Anderson, J. A. (Eds.), I*dentity meets nationality: Voices from the Humanities* (pp. 242-264). Accra: Sub-Saharan Publishers.

Arnheim, R. (1970). Gestalt psychology. *Art Journal*. 30 (1), 85

Asiedu, M.A. (2014). 'Introduction'. In Asiedu, M.A, Collins, J., Gbormittah, F. and Nii Yartey, F. (Eds.), *The performing arts in Africa- Ghanaian perspectives: An introduction* (p. 1-9). Oxfordshire: Ayebia Clarke Publishing Limited.

Barber, K. (1987). Popular arts in Africa. *African Arts Review*, 10(3), 1-78.

Bell, S. (2009). 'The academic mode of production'. In Smith, H. and Dean, R. T. (eds.), *Practice-led research, research-led practice, in the creative arts* (p. 252-263). Edinburgh: Edinburgh University Press.

Blom, L.A. and Chaplin, L. T. (1982). The intimate act of choreography. Pittsburgh: University of Pittsburgh Press.

Carlson, N. R. and Heath, C. D. (2010). *Psychology the Science of Behaviour*, Ontario, CA: Pearson Education Canada.

Dodds, S. (2009). From Busby Berkeley to Madonna: Music Video and Popular Dance. In Malnig, J. (Ed.) Ballroom, boogie, shimmy sham, shake: A social and popular dance reader. Urbana and Chicago. IL: University of Illinois press.

Eagleton, Terry. (1996). *Literary theory an introduction* (2nd ed.) Oxford & Victoria: Blackwell Publishing.

Gyekye, K. (2013) *Philosophy, Culture and vision: African perspectives*. Accra: Sub-Saharan Publishers

Hargoe, A.N. and Salifu, J.T. (2014). 'Dance in worship: The disposition of Islam and Christianity'. In Awo Asiedu, M.A., Collins, J., Gbormittah, F. and Nii Yartey, F., (Eds.) *The performing arts in Africa- Ghanaian perspectives: An introduction* (p. 88-95). Oxfordshire: Ayebia Clarke Publishing Limited.

Manuh, T. and Sutherland-Addy, E. (2013). 'Introduction'. In Manuh, T. and Sutherland-Addy, E. (Eds.), *Africa in contemporary perspective: A textbook for Undergraduate Students* (p. 1-12). Accra: Sub-Saharan Publishers.

Martin, J. (1965). *The Dance in Theory*. New Jersey: Princeton Book Company Publishers.

Nii-Yartey, F. (2016). *African Dance in Ghana: Contemporary transformations*. London: Mot Juste Limited.

Nii-Yartey, F. (2006). 'Dance symbolism in Africa'. In Manuh, T., and Sutherland-Addy, E., (Eds.) *Africa in contemporary perspective: A textbook for undergraduate students* (pp. 413-429). Accra: Sub-Saharan Publishers.

Obeng, S. (1997). *Selected Speeches of Nkrumah*. Accra: Afram Publications (Ghana) Limited.

Ofosu, T.B.K. and Sowah, Oh! N. K. (2014). 'Dancing to words, ideas and rhymes'. In Awo Asiedu, M.A. Collins, J., Gbormittah, F., and Nii Yartey, F. (Eds.) *The performing arts in Africa- Ghanaian perspectives: An introduction* (p. 109-122). Oxfordshire: Ayebia Clarke Publishing Limited.

Ofosu, T.B.K. and Deh T. (2015). 'The azonto dance, A Ghanaian new creation: Exploring new boundaries of popular dance forms'. *African Performance Review*. 9 (1): 45-64

Ofosu, T.B.K. (2009). 'A synthesis of popular and scholarly choreography: Dance aesthetics and current trends in Ghana'. *Unpublished Thesis*. Princeton Department of Dance Studies University of Ghana, Legon.

Okpewho,I. (1992). *African Oral Literature*. Bloomington and Indianapolis: Indian University Press.

Reynolds, Larry. (2003). 'Early representatives.' In Reynolds L. and Herman-Kinney, N. (eds). Handbook of Symbolic Interactionism (pp. 59–81). Alta Mira.

Saah, K.K. & Baaku, K. (2011). "Do not rob us of ourselves' language and nationalism in colonial Ghana'. In Lauer, H., Amfo, N. A. A. and Anderson, J. A. (Eds.), *Identity meets nationality: Voices from the Humanities*. Accra: Sub-Saharan Publishers.

Smith-Aurtard, M. J. (2000, 4th ed.). *Dance composition*. New York: Routledge.

Waskul, D. and Vannini, P. (2006). 'Introduction: The Body in Symbolic Interaction'. In Wskul, D., and Vannini P., (eds.), *Body/ Embodiment: Symbolic Interactionism and Sociology of the Body* (pp. 1-18). Hampshire and Burlington: Ashgate Publishing Company.

FOOTNOTE

1. Kwame Nkrumah's speech during the opening of the Institute of African Studies at the University of Ghana, Legon, 25 October 1963.

2. A derogatory terminology coined from the traditional drum Donno that was often used in performances of music, dance and drama at the School of Performing Arts during its inception. 'Dondology' is still very much prevalent presently in the Ghanaian parlance.

FREESTYLE

KENDRICK 'H2O' SANDY

Breathe... breathe... breathe...
feel the beat...
breathe... breathe... breathe...
stay on beat ...
breathe and allow the music to talk,
musicality talk back let the conversation
take you, take you, take you.

You take, you take that energy,
you take that moment all is watching
and no-one is there,
all is watching and no-one is there
it's all you,
it's all me, it's all you,
it's all me, me, you,
just you, the music,
the conversation,
so let's talk the conversation,
so let's talk ...
the conversation so let's talk.

I'm listening, I'm listening, I'm listening,
the matrix, the matrix, the matrix.
I'm listening, the matrix, the matrix,
the matrix.
I am listening. I am listening,
the matrix, the matrix, the matrix...

Freestyling, that's what I'm on. That kind of vibe, spontaneity, that something can change. I started dancing in September 1998. Was I into dance? No, I was not into dance. I wanted to do sports, and art and design. Dance was for girls. I was ignorant, a Black guy who just wanted to do sports, play basketball and football.

I use to play basketball in a sports hall in East London. They had a café upstairs, where my best friend, my brother, and my girlfriend were hanging out. They were freestyling, doing their routines and dancing. I'm downstairs bowling, I'm dumping on people, I'm getting dumped by people. I'm trying to check my game. Then we go upstairs to have some water and I have a look and see what's going on. They are jumping around and I think that it looks cool. I see some breaking - that looks masculine. I can do a cartwheel, I can do flips. I can bust that move.

Then I hear about doing a performance at The 291 Club.

Up until that point, I could do my tricks, I could do my flips, I could do a little break-dancing. Then I'm told *"Ken, the only thing is you have to learn a routine"*. I'm directed to an 11-year-old girl (I was 18 years old at the time). I watch the foundation. Thinking *"Finally, I will get the routine."*

I did that performance. Now that spontaneity. That moment of improvising. Going on like I knew what I was doing. I didn't know nothing. What I did know was that there was this energy. There was this thing that I wanted to do. Something there that made me say to myself *"hold on, something's pulling."*

It completely changed my whole career. I went from doing art and design to doing a performing arts course. Contemporary dance, not ballet, not jazz, not tap. But contemporary was a bit abstract, because you could let yourself go. It's kind of like the rebel of ballet. I can do what I want to do and my body's going to move in a particular way. I do a little hip hop. And I'm a Black guy. The only Black guy that is on the course. The only undergraduate on the course. So, I decide to do hip hop. Everyone else is doing contemporary, ballet, and I am trying to feed the five thousand.

Life is made up of all these little moments. I have all these different situations in my life. Everything feels like freestyle, because everything's going so quick. Moving so quick you don't know what's going on, you can't structure it.

In another moment, at Stratford Shopping Centre, I go to do a show as part of a summer school. I have my own crew. I can do a couple of moves so do a couple of moves. I'm asked if we can open the show. Stratford Shopping Centre is a place where everyone goes; all my old schoolfriends are there. I'm in that moment. I've been practicing for it. I've come to the point in the music when I'm ready. I'm freestyling. I run, I flip, I land, life changes from basketball, art and design to dance, changing everything.

So why am I saying all of this? For me it was all freestyle. Life made it freestyle. The situation and scenarios made it freestyle. So, when we're talking about identity and choreographic practice - it was that moment at that summer school at Stratford Shopping Centre that gave me an identity. It gave me confidence, it empowered me, it gave me motivation.

Following the show, kids in the area said that they wanted to dance. We did an audition and facilitated, supported and mentored starting up a youth group. People wanted it, so we made it happen.

There was no business plan, no SWOT analysis. But what there was were people who wanted to dance. That to me is freestyle. That to me is improvisation. It is life. You wake up in the morning, you don't know what's going to happen; you don't know what is going to happen when you leave that door in the morning. You improvise. You miss the bus, you have to improvise. You run after the bus. That doesn't work, you have to try and call a cab. You keep trying to find a way to get where you need to be.

Another time I was with my friend Mikey J. I was at his house jam and had a rum and coke or two. There was a battle, a dance battle. I'm facing this guy and we had a little rivalry. I had beat him and I beat him again. But, this time I've given him an advantage, as I was a little bit tipsy. He's there trying to bust his moves, feel the beats. In that moment, I'm trying to create structure. I'm trying to choreograph myself in order to make sure that I'm ready for him. To make sure I'm ready that moment, ready for that time…

When it comes to teaching I think that we have to make sure that we have some form of a teaching tool, a language. If I'm going to be a part of this hip hop thing, I'm going to be a part of this culture, this greenhouse. I need to feel everything. I need to feed everything. I need to be able to show to the kids that I'm not just one of those teachers that's just talking. They will be more motivated and inspired if they see me doing it too. I make sure I go and do a commercial drop. Then when I come back, even when it is same time as rehearsals, I'm going to go to battle. That's my culture. That's my scene. That's my life. So, we created our own language. I want the young people I work with to understand structure, and then play within that structure. From there we create our own grooves, our movement, our own routines. Some of these are routines that must be ten years old, that we teach young kids again so they can learn.

We make our own boy grooves and blues routines abbreviation. Three letters for grooves and movement and four letters for routines. Then I can send a message on WhatsApp with the combination. I am starting to create a structure. It's maths, it's science, putting in the equations. I think it's important to put in a structure. Right now, from a hip hop point of view, there are so many people with their opinions and politics. I don't care for the politics, what I care about is the dance and how it makes me feel. Having this structure, this language, gives me something to refer back to. Am I going to use this move, or am I going to change it? I can make sure people understand what I'm doing. I want to educate myself to make sure I can educate others. If we create a structure, a system that's going to help others to understand something, they can take that system and do what they want with it. Hip hop is something that you take and you make it your own.

Then we can start thinking about space. We can create different formats like the nine-step walk. Imagine nine squares in front of you. From those nine squares put your hand on one, put your hand on five, put your hand on seven… You have already learned some kind of sequence. Advance that further and go into a fifty-four-square cube. You can start to play with the matrix. There are so many different spaces we can work with, to play with, and improvise with. Two X's represent your feet. The line represents the direction you are facing. One you put your hands up, two you go over there, three to the side, four down and so on… You can create little things from play that you can start using from an education point of view and we are still using this in schools, for education. Playing with these spaces, my dynamic starts to change. I can use it for freestyle, I can use it for choreography. I can use it for play.

My matrix is three different things: emotion, motion and music. Emotion is how I feel at that time. I'm vexed, I'm making something because I'm vexed, but if I'm happy I'm making something because I'm happy. *What is the music telling me? how does it make me feel?* The motion. *What are the motions? Is it a lock and turn?* I want to be honest with myself so if I'm going to make something it has to be honest, organic and real. I take a moment to think about what I want to relay to someone else, so I freestyle. I play around and then when I like it, I keep it, and make that into a structure and that structure to me is choreography, structured freestyle.

So, what is my practice? My practice is freestyle, my practice is emotion, my practice is being motionless and being motional, emotional. Using movement and playing with that and being motive, provocative, emotive. You have to have everything for it all to come together.

COLONIAL PASTS: NEW AESTHETICS

THE ROOTS AND ROUTES OF AFRICAN/ NEO-AFRICAN DANCE PRACTICE AND TRAINING

'H' PATTEN

INTRODUCTION

The influence of culture and training on my choreographic vocabulary, how identity is revealed through practice, and the influence of colonial pasts and new aesthetics are the challenges this paper seeks to address. In researching the genealogy of Jamaican Dancehall, I am aware that a simple chronology of my training and choreographic works is insufficient for such a task. Through my research, I have become acutely conscious of the many contextual influences that collide in shaping the decisions and directions individuals may take in negotiating the life-cycle events that shape the roots and routes of identity, agency and personhood, through African/ 'neo-African' (meaning new diasporic African; Ryman, 1984) dance practice and training.

The question I ask is why should others be interested in my artistic development? Perhaps it's because it foregrounds some key issues surrounding the development of African and Caribbean dance practice, or as currently termed in the UK, Dance of the African Diaspora (DAD). Importantly, it may offer some insight to both emerging and other established artists, about how they might approach their own artistic practice, ideas and personal career development. Hence, this paper seeks to provide a brief genealogical exploration, meaning a presentation of the connections and/or collisions between dance, cultural heritage, identity and professional development, as manifested within my own choreographic practice and training within African and Caribbean arts.

Incorporating an auto/ethnographic approach with participant observation, in this paper I will first outline how identity relates to my choreographic approach in relation to my first production Ina De Wildanis (1992). I will contextualise the social and political background out of which I created the work and the multifaceted relationship between identity and choreography. My choreographic training will be presented in relation to the Elements (2001) collaboration with Ghanaian choreographer Professor Francis Nii-Yartey, to demonstrate the impact of culture and training within both the African and British framework. Finally, using The Cotton Tree Passage (2010) as a catalyst I will outline some barriers that exist for aspiring choreographers within African and Caribbean dance.

IDENTITY AND CHOREOGRAPHY – INA DE WILDANIS

January 1992, in a hotel room in Lusaska (Zambia), I woke in the middle of the night. Turning on the light, I reached for a pen and paper, desperately trying to retain the images or 'visions' I had dreamt, before they disappeared forever. I quickly wrote down notes of the vision and references hidden within my dream. This was the beginning of my first solo show.

Later, I jumped out of my sleep again, I fumbled for a pen and paper, then quickly turning on the light, scribbled down more notes, part two of the vision. This continued throughout the night. As daylight broke, I awoke exhausted, but excited as I wrote down the final act. Ina De Wildanis was now fully conceived. Nigerian choreographer Amatu Dabeye Braid would classify this as 'dream state' visions, as to become choreography, an artist has 'to bring in something which is different from known possession movements' (in Moyo, 1995 p.17), as I later did.

Following a six-week rehearsal period, the vision opened, Ina De Wildanis (IDW), my first one-man show, charting the search for identity and home, transporting audiences from Africa to the Caribbean and to Europe. Ina De Wildanis featured dance, prose, storytelling, integrated song and dance, puppetry, masquerade and carnivalesque costume. Additionally, as music and dance are inextricably linked within African/neo-African practices, I incorporated three live musicians. This significantly impacted on my creative process. Much of the rehearsal period was spent composing and developing the music for dances such as Likishi, Vimbuza, and Gule Wam Kulu. These forms were unknown to the musicians as this was the first time they would be presented in 'spectacular' (theatrical) form in the UK. As a solo artist, the production forced me to draw on all aspects of myself, my roots (cultural heritage) and the routes of my identity.

IDENTITY THROUGH ARTISTIC PRACTICE

The above anecdote relates to identity generally and to my personal background, growing up in Birmingham within a strong Jamaican community, where I gained a solid sense of identity through cultural expression. As outlined in *'Feel De Riddim, Feel De Vibes: dance as a transcendent act of survival and upliftment',* (Adair and Burt, 2016), born twenty days after my mother's arrival in the UK, I grew up through the 1960s, 70s and 80s attending Jamaican social events, weddings, 'birth-night' parties and christenings, which all featured dance as the main and often concluding event. I attended the Pentecostal Church from childhood, which fed both my cultural and spiritual roots. The spiritual and cultural roots and routes of African/neo-African dance maintain an important and integral role in the development of both my identity and dance practice.

Visions such as those described in the development of Ina De Wildanis have and continue to form the catalyst for much of my choreography and associated creative expression. They serve as examples and extensions of my cultural heritage, one in which individuals pay special attention to dreams, visions, the senses and 'feelings' (spiritual connections and/or disconnections).

Dianne M Stewart (2005 p.xii) cites her mother in asserting, 'psychic powers are evinced through dreams', which are regarded as crucial elements within the intuitive development of individuals. Most Jamaican elders habitually speak of their 'spirit' (the innate sense or judgement of character) either taking to, or not taking to another person, or situation, forming an important part of one's intuitive development.

Ina De Wildanis speaks to my own intuitive development, as the central image displays my face behind the mask, alluding to the fact that it is the human spirit that animates the dance mask, yet behind it the dancer's corporeality is performative (Butler, 1988; Nash, 2000) that is, constructed behavioural actions that project a persona behind which is concealed another, that is animated by the ancestors and ultimately, the Supreme Being. Kariamu Welsh rightly asserts, 'African dance is theater in that it involves song, drama, masquerade traditions, and music' (2010, p.16). Ina De Wildanis utilises dance, combining the associated arts practices it theatrically embodies, focusing on masquerade and spiritual practices to convey meaning. Laura S. Grillo suggests, 'Masking's dynamic medium vividly appeals to its spectators to embrace the worldview that it depicts' (2012, p.116). Masquerade highlights the multifaceted relationship between identity and culture in my choreography, which function alongside the spiritual dances to foreground the relationship between the dancer and the viewer, the material and the spiritual worlds, as Dianne M Stewart's (2005) study outlines. Randolph-Dalton Hyman (2012) presents a roll call of African Caribbean scholars from Germaine Acogny, Rex Nettleford and Pearl Primus to Omofolabo Soyinka Ajayi amongst many others who support the functional role of dance within the African context.

Ina De Wildanis functions as a window into the worldviews that many African/neo-African youths, and I, unconsciously employ in contemporary Britain. Thus, it foregrounds the *'in-between'* (Bhabha, 1994) nature of the space many occupy in Britain, and therefore signifies the masquerade many youths construct for their survival.

The DJ/scholar Lez Henry, aptly summarises youth survival behaviour as, a *'"performance" that outwardly masks an inner reality'* (2002 p.51), which I suggest assists their negotiation of the in-between *'countercultural'* (Beckford, 2006) wilderness in which they reside. As Ina De Wildanis foregrounds, this results in the holding of incomplete sets of keys to multiple identities — African, African Caribbean and UK.

Within my own upbringing I was made acutely aware of the lack of status of Black communities through the marginalisation of Black youths and the strained relations between Black identity, police and state authority. The overtly racist treatment of Black people was common across most aspects of British life prior to the Race Relations Act (1976) and the Equality Act (2010). Robert Beckford's Jamaican Bible Remix (2017) music project, draws on testimonials from African and African Caribbean elders who encountered signs stating, 'No dogs, no Irish, no blacks', when searching for housing on their arrival in Britain. 'Sonny's Lettah' (1979) by dub poet Linton Kwesi Johnson (LKJ) further portrays the brutalising oppression many Black youths experienced under the 'SUS law', empowering police arrests of individuals 'suspected of loitering with intent to commit an arrestable offence' (BBC News Thursday, 14 December, 2000). The precursor to the current 'Stop and Search' law, as a yute (youth) it was implemented against me on several occasions.

Experiences such as these served to 'other' African and African Caribbean communities and engendered feelings of 'outsiderness' within Britain's dominant white society. In response, many Black youths explored identity through the political ideologies of the growing Rastafarian movement emerging out of 1970s Jamaica, building on the earlier Civil Rights Movement in the USA and the Black Power Movement both sides of the Atlantic. Rastafari transferred to Britain through reggae music and assisted the establishment of 'smadditisation' (Mills 1997) or personhood for many British based Black youths.

The 1970s and 80s socio-political experiences collided to make my involvement in dance both a political and cultural development strategy. Ina De Wildanis therefore manifested as an embodied outpouring and a reinforcement of identity through dance, as exemplified by my LKJ inspired, 'Dear Mamma' message home, leading into the Pentecostal Church section. Created using a contemporised Zulu 'Warrior' dance 'Isigi Seven' step, comprising of seven footsteps — jumping forward on the right, bringing left together, right touch out, in, left touch out, in, right step back, with the body rippling, whilst mirroring the feet — I incorporated the Rastafarian 'Nyabinghi' dance break, featuring a — crouching forward and back weight shifting movement, flat footed, left, right jog, into a staccato front to back alternating stamp to the riddim (rhythm), 'pam, pa-tam, pa-tam, silence, bam!' — the concluding stamp, symbolised youthful exuberance, alongside the ideological strength and resistant survival of 1990s African Caribbean youths!

African dance therefore served not only as an aesthetic expression, but contributed to a sense of smadditisation and identity for most Black youths participating in the genre. Additionally, it helped to further cultivate the cultural and socio-political consciousness of many early African Caribbean practitioners, myself included. African and Caribbean dance was totally embedded within the Black community, reliant on their support to develop initial audience bases. My personal route into workshop participation and watching African/neo-African dance performances was often linked to socio-political events and initiatives such as Afro People's Organisation (Birmingham), African Liberation Day celebrations (national) and community festivals featuring performances by Lanzel African Arts (Wolverhampton), led by Chester Morrison and Ekome Dance Company (Bristol), established by Barry Anderson, and the many companies that later emerged in the East and West Midlands. However, as Bob Ramdhanie rightly contends in conversation, many within Britain's Black communities did not necessarily welcome an association with their African heritage, as some felt assimilation was the route necessary to avoid racial tensions.

CHOREOGRAPHIC PRACTICE

Within my choreographic practice, I deliberately exploit the multifaceted relationship between identity and choreography, embodying African/neo-African historical, contemporary and urban lived experiences. As part of what I am developing as the 'Korotech' technique, I implement an approach to choreography that combines the Caribbean classification of dance practices, namely: African retention; Creolised or indigenous practices; and European influenced forms. The first is represented by the extraction of dance vocabulary from the artists or participants I work with, forming their personal expression. The second aspect is what is created collaboratively with participants through the exchange of ideas and the manipulation, fusion and development of new dance vocabulary. The third element is the African/neo-African vocabulary that I impart or teach, thereby imposing material on the artists and/or participants I work with, in subverting and replicating the European imposition on African forbears.

The Korotech approach simultaneously combines the identity of those I work with and that of myself, reflecting identity as being a continual process of becoming, as revealed choreographically and in my teaching/delivery processes. The combining of identity with multiple art forms and technical skills through the choreographic process not only extends individual creativity but also makes the collaborative process possible and enriched, as I shall now detail.

CHOREOGRAPHY AND TRAINING – ELEMENTS

In February 2001, whilst in transit to Burkina Faso, I spent two nights in Ghana, hosted by Professor Francis Nii-Yartey, under whom I trained with Ghana Dance Ensemble, the then National Company, in 1982. Nii-Yartey introduced me to his own company, NOYAM African Dance Institute, established to enable him to experiment and develop contemporary African dance. Through NOYAM, Nii-Yartey choreographically 'negotiates between the old traditions and the impulses and issues of Africa's new generation' (Nii-Yartey, 2016, p.35), alongside fulfilling his national brief, directing the Ghana National Dance Company.

The National Dance Company foregrounds dance as representing culture as the way of life of a particular people, period or group. Thereby, 'culture' becomes property, but also remains plural, belonging to a nation, community or group above and beyond the individual (Williams, 1976). Relating to Noyam, 'culture' represents intellectual artistic expression and, as such, a distinction is often drawn between high-art and what many perceive as popular or low-culture (ibid). This reflects the distinction between those within and those outside the dominant ruling class structures. In the British context, this distinction has historically been explicitly clear in the tensions existing between the funding structures and the '*African and Caribbean dance sector, commonly termed "Black Dance" or African People's Dance (APD)*' (Patten in Adair and Burt, 2016, p.115). Now more commonly termed 'Dance of the African Diaspora' (DAD), the constant re-defining of the sector to suit socio-politico-economic trends exemplifies the impact of power dynamics.

Returning to the Elements collaboration, Nii invited me to spend a couple of days to, as he remarked: *"Experiment with Noyam and see what can come out"* (Nii-Yartey in conversation 2001). There was a sharing of ideas and creativity. Working with Nii and Noyam allowed me to push boundaries and free myself of many of the restrictions and confines enforced on artistic creation within the African dance idiom in Britain. I will expand on this shortly. Ideas developed – a short two-minute 'dance for camera' pilot was created and the Elements project was born.

The Elements research and development period provided the opportunity and luxury for me to work with an ensemble of dancers already trained within the African dance idiom and possessing an in-depth knowledge of the traditions they had grown up with and/or learnt. This allowed me to experiment with the 'inner dancer', tapping into the depths of their emotions and experiences in order to draw out movement vocabulary. Marrying both traditional and contemporary urban responses to the lived experiences of the dancers and myself, facilitated a departure from 'set' traditional movement vocabulary.

The process of creating the Elements mask dance section exemplifies the creative 'inner dancer' process. The dancer and I worked towards tapping into 'the artist within' (Merle Van Den Bosch, in conversation, 1990s). I gave him vocab, which he eagerly learnt; he then shared vocab from his traditional background and we extended the boundaries of both, weaving them together to create new movement vocabulary. However, in his first masquerade performance, on entering the stage wearing the mask, he was greeted with laughter and playfulness, instead of an air of fear and/or mysticism. This signalled to me the need for further artistic development, despite the dancer's belief that the audience's claps and cheers signified a successful performance.

Going back to the beginning, we again exchanged dance vocabulary. Working back and forth in creating the dance, I explained that the audience's laughter indicated a misinterpretation of the function of the masquerade dance, despite appreciative applauses. He worked and I pushed him deeper within himself. The musicians played and the male dancers sang. Finally, he felt sufficiently practiced at accessing his deeper consciousness.

Music playing, he began the dance. He shook hands with each musician and dancer, one by one. As he slammed his hand against mine, clapping and shaking it, I immediately felt his power and knew he had gone into the 'myal' possession state. The ancestral spirits had arrived and taken control of him. His brother grew concerned but the music continued and the spirit danced, mixing West African, Ghanaian Ewe dance movements, involving – *the forward and back (contract and release) action of the Agbadza (A-ba-ja) chest movement* – with Caribbean dance vocabulary, including Jamaican Revivalism, featuring – *the forward stamp of the foot, initiated by the forward lunge and twist of the shoulder, before both shoulder and foot is pulled back to the starting position to repeat again* – and the Haitian Yanvalou, comprising of – *the circling action of alternating feet on the ground, as if trapping the spirit* – the new masquerade dance emerged. The dance ended but the spirit remained in him!

His brother and fellow Ghanaians took charge, believing they best knew what to do. Try as they might, the spirit refused to leave. I then took over, collecting "likkle dis, likkle dat" (a little of this and a little of that) as my aunty always remarks when preparing traditional healing remedies. I implemented things I had witnessed African/neo-African practitioners using/doing in this situation. I held him and talked to him. He slowly came back to himself. The artists all enquired, "How did you know what to do?" To this day, I do not recall what I said and did, but I informed them that the ancestral spirits within him had been a mixture of both his and mine, each set making different demands. However, once satisfied, all ancestors had departed. The dancer adopted a more serious approach to his execution of the dance. The following performances brought further possession, standing ovations, fear, exhilaration, growth and finally 'overstanding', the Rastafarian ideological term meaning and replacing understanding. Importantly, the masquerade dance provided the performer with smadditisation, the sense of self-worth and agency.

AFRICAN AND CARIBBEAN DANCE IN BRITAIN

Within the British context, training in African and Caribbean dance has historically been routed through the companies, with individual leaders and/or choreographers delivering their distinctive style and approach to their members. My original training in Ghana under Nii-Yartey furnished me with a good foundational introduction to choreography, and therefore the freedom to explore and be creative within the African dance idiom. The Black Dance Development Trust's (BDDT) five annual summer-school courses played an important role in further building and developing the choreographic skills and training within a fledgling sector. Delivered by amongst others Sheila Barnett (Jamaica), C. K. Ladzepko (Ghana), Albert Mawere Opoku (Ghana), Francis Nii-Yartey (Ghana), Mbye Chow (The Gambia), Mariama Ngome (Senegal), Patsy Ricketts (Jamaica), Jackie Guy (Jamaica) and Peter Badejo (Nigeria), these artists shared their choreographic approaches in formal choreography classes.

Conversely, others such as George Dzikunu (Ghana), Elliott Ngubane (South Africa), Jeanette Springer (Trinidad and Tobago), Monty Williams (Grenada) and others, shared choreographic approaches indirectly, through the process of choreographing on participants.

I personally learnt much of my choreographic techniques by memorising the approach and stages choreographers went through whilst choreographing on me.

The distinction between a dance 'choreographer' and a 'dance arranger' was one of the many issues hotly debated within the BDDT summer-school courses. Some choreographers used set traditional dance movements in their original form, creating new floor patterns and therefore new relationships between the dance artists, musicians and audiences. Yet, as they never actually created 'new' movement vocabulary themselves, some argued they should be classified as 'dance arrangers'. Those who attempted to add, subtract, extend and push the boundaries of the actual steps or movement vocabulary were argued as being true choreographers. Yet, they also ran the risk of being accused of bastardising the traditional dances, as I expand upon relating to the UK context.

BARRIERS TO CREATIVE EXPRESSION

As apprentices, UK artists were taught most of the African dances as 'set' movement vocabulary, which have existed for and been passed down over many generations. Thereby, some traditionalists view any changes or alterations to the ancient African dance steps, as dilution and/or bastardisation, rather than the creative development of the forms. I witnessed much criticism of Nii-Yartey's early works, as he dared to alter, change, and create on the Ghanaian traditional movements. However, now regarded as a national treasure, prior to his untimely departure to the realm of the ancestors, Nii-Yartey was awarded the highest accolade by the Ghanaian government. Nii-Yartey also directed the highest profiling national and international events, including the opening and closing ceremonies for football's 'All Africa Games'.

For many years I used Caribbean dance vocabulary as my creative tool to experiment and develop new movement vocabulary and choreography. I maintained the arrangement mode for African dance, particularly in relation to Ghanaian dances, for some time. However, as I developed the Korotech approach to dance, encouraged by Nii-Yartey, Ladzepko, Nettleford, Welsh-Asante and others, I found the confidence and freedom to truly explore and create within both the African and Caribbean genres. This now facilitates my synthesising of both forms. I describe the resultant creative expression elsewhere:

"My own practice, from 'Inna De Wildanis' (1991) to 'The Cotton Tree Passage' (2010), all reflect and signal the spiritual underpinning of African/neo-African dance, including the dancehall phenomenon. ['The Cotton Tree Passage'] combining Revivalism and dancehall movements ... [performed to] veteran DJ Spragga Benz's specially commissioned track, re-working the sound of enslavement and/or emotively foregrounding the dungeon soundscape ... [t]he Revival balancing step – one foot stepping out, the other brought to meet it – morphs into dancehall's Summer Bounce, where the pelvis scribes backwards half-circles to an upright break/stop, on alternating sides. The drilling step – crouching, sideways rocking, [with] alternating, foot stamping – develops into dancehall's Tek weh yuself – sharp pelvic and knee twist, throwing the arm out in the opposite direction.

These symbolisms underscore my practice, permitting spiritually embodied ancestral data and cultural knowledge to manifest a cultural memory that connects the riddim and vibe of both church hall and dancehall space."

(Patten, in Adair, 2016, p.119)

Although The Cotton Tree Passage enabled greater choreographic freedom and experimentation, it also highlighted some of the serious challenges within African dance. Due to the vastness of the African continent, many different approaches exist towards choreography, with different catalysts facilitating the creative process. Thereby, many dancers may not necessarily be schooled in the style of movement a particular African and African Caribbean choreographer requires. Choreographers are therefore obliged to first teach their required dance vocabulary, drill that vocabulary to allow the dancer's bodies to receive and accept it, before finally being able to choreograph. This greatly impacts on rehearsal schedules, as a six-week choreographic rehearsal may become three weeks teaching and drilling, leaving less than three weeks for the actual choreographic process.

Dance within the African context is functional, as Doris Green (in Hyman, 2012) and others rightly assert. Yet, many dancers are frequently unaware of the meaning behind much of the movement vocabulary within their repertoire. This therefore forces choreographers to find time to interpret their movement for the artists involved in their dance pieces, in order to ensure the correct intent and meanings are executed throughout the entire piece, in creating a successful product. This extends beyond the dance, because as earlier highlighted, additional rehearsal time must be devoted to the composing and rehearsing of the music and musicians. The use of verbal utterance is therefore a vital tool for African and African Caribbean dance choreographers.

I have used verbal utterance in recreating dancehall riddims on drums and through corporeal dancing bodies, whilst collaborating with master musicians and dancers, in combining the music and dance. Hence, African Caribbean choreographers are often forced to reproduce or compose the music to varying degrees and impart the 'vibe' (feeling) required, whilst simultaneously creating movement vocabulary.

CONCLUSION

In this paper, I have shown Ina De Wildanis through its research period and creation, as representing an example of the narrative form of African dance theatre, thematically depicting the root and routes of African/neo-African dance. Elements and The Cotton Tree Passage both represent the ideological thematic development and integration of contemporary African and Caribbean dance vocabulary, with particular aspects of the process serving as an initiation process for the artists and participants I collaborate and work with.

With its traditional 'root' source, my work allows me to explore how the body communicates messages both physically and spiritually, as a transmitter, sending and receiving symbolic meaning. Why does this matter? Culture and identity have a deep significance that embodies African/neo-African spiritual cosmology and religious coding as part of contemporary Black artistic expression in Britain, the Caribbean and Africa. The dancing body draws on these roots and routes, facilitating the acquisition, sharing and development of ancestral data, cultural knowledge and cultural memory.

REFERENCES

BBC News (2000) 'The Power to Stop and Search'.
14 December *BBC News*. Available at:
http://news.bbc.co.uk/1/hi/uk/1070552.stm
(Accessed: 22 November 2017)

Beckford, R. (2006) *Jesus Dub: Theology, Music
and Social Change*. Routledge. Oxon OX; USA and
Canada New York, NY

Bhabha, H. K. (1994) *The Location of Culture*. Routledge.

Braid, A. D. (1995) *Pan-Essent-Move africa95 International
Dance Workshop: 7-17 March 1995*, Safari Lodge, Victoria
Falls, Zimbabwe. Produced by africa95 in association with
The British Council Zimbabwe.

Butler, J. (1988) *Performative Acts and Gender Constitution:
An Essay in Phenomenology and Feminist Theory*.
Theatre Journal, Vol. 40, No. 4., pp. 519-531.

Grillo, L. S. (2012) 'African Ritual' in Bongmba, E. K. (Ed.)
The Wiley-Blackwell companion to African religions. Malden,
MA, Wiley-Blackwell.

Henry W. L. (2002) *Reggae/dancehall music: the 'hidden
voice' of Black British urban expression*. PhD Dissertation.
University of London.

Hyman, R-D. (2012) *Daggering Inna Di Dancehall:
Kierkegaard's Conceptualisation of Subjectivity and
Nietzsche's Dionysus in Relation to Jamaican Dance*.
Simon Fraser University PhD.

Mills, C. (1997). 'Smadditizin': *Caribbean Quarterly Volume*
43:2, pp. 54-68

Nash, C. (2000). *Performativity in practice: some recent
work in cultural geography. Progress in Human Geography*
24,4 (2000) pp. 653–664

Nii-Yartey F. (2016) *African Dance in Ghana: Contemporary
Transformations*. Mot Juste Limited. UK.

Patten, H. (2016) 'Feel De Riddim, Feel De Vibes: dance
as a transcendent act of survival and upliftment'. In: Adair, C.
and Burt, R. *British Dance: Black routes*. Routledge, Oxon,
New York

Ryman, C. (1984)' Jonkonnu: a Neo-African Form',
Jamaica Journal Vol 17, No 1 pp.13-27.

Stewart, D. M. (2005) *Three Eyes for the Journey:
African Dimensions of the Jamaican Religious Experience*.
Oxford University Press.

Welsh, K. (2010) *African Dance, World of Dance Second
Edition*. Infobase Publishing.

Williams, R. (1976, 1983) *Keywords: A vocabulary of culture
and society*. Revised edition, Fontana Paperbacks, London.

DANCE EXPLORATION THROUGH REGGAE MOVES

DAVID HAMILTON

Identity and choreographic practice. How did this happen for me? When I was 15 years old, in Leeds, at Intake High School (now West Park Academy) I had to choreograph a solo performance for my dance exam. When it came to music choice, students would usually dip into the teachers' vast music collection. I made a decision, I wanted to express myself the way I was at home, and the music I listened to was reggae music. I did my solo to *Africa* by The Mighty Diamonds. All I knew at the time, all I wanted to do, was to express myself. I worked hard at school, I wouldn't be the dancer I am today without it, but how I learnt how to express myself that did not come directly from my contemporary dance teachers. That came from my parents, from my community. I would say I am a reggae contemporary dancer. It does not mean that I'm not happy with anything else, far from it. (Years ago, I choreographed *Blues in the Night* for Peepul Centre in Leicester, which is Jazz. I worked at Bradford Opera in the 90s.) But if you asked me to express my soul, no competition, this is the music. Reggae. At the time, it was just a decision I made, I didn't even realise how important it was to become for my career.

I went to London School of Contemporary Dance, for one year to learn Graham Technique. I had six years of Laban from school. A lot of the dancers from Leeds, Black dancers, all remember their routines from school.Movement stimulus was the primary teaching method and choreographic basis of school dance productions.

The method of movement stimulus empowered students to be creative, imaginative and receptive as individuals. That was what it came to with the productions that we did at the time. The better the class, the better the productions.

One of the things in the relationship to school, instead of someone giving you the ideas, you are now the initiator of the ideas. The development from school and the difference with Phoenix was the dancers were now the givers of the movement ideas and choreographers, self contained. This development and difference is important to understanding the dance foundation of Phoenix, which has two foundations, one is dance in schools and the other dance from the community. This experience became the foundation of Phoenix Dance Company. We went away to Spain and when we came back afterwards it came to this dance, this dance is called *The Story of the Phoenix*.

Jump ahead to RJC Dance. I didn't seriously start to think about reggae in any serious way until RJC Dance. RJC means: reggae, jazz and contemporary. I represent the R side, Edward Lynch represents the J, Donald Edwards represents the C. It was not till RJC that I seriously started to think about developing reggae. For example, I used to teach a class so I took something very simple, rock reggae, sometimes it became looser, then instead of doing a dip, I took a rock step (as we called it) and used that as the basis of something else. We were developing our own exercises. It was not until RJC that I seriously started to think about teaching that way, and choreographing that way. I could see which people I could work with.

In around 2002, I made a decision about the direction of reggae. I left RJC and started Reggeyeshun Dance Theatre. One of the first big projects was on Bob Marley. Looking at Bob Marley as a dancer, the word we would use to describe what he does is skankin. When he is performing there are certain steps he changed. You would only know that if you knew what skanking was. Observing Bob Marley in a particular show that he did, we transformed some of those movements into a piece of choreography to show how Bob Marley danced, how he had danced in a said way.

As a choreographer, naturally you want to express different ideas and sometimes experience that in a sense of negotiating the style of dance and wanting to use it in theatre and also bringing in your own experience. Bob Marley had done a track which was in honour of his father and, with the loss of my mother, I wanted to honour her. Also, people like to talk about folk, folk and reggae comes along with nyabinghi which I use in the nature of my work.

I used the track *Mother Earth by Bushman*. If you listen to the lyrics it says more than it is. It's very much about the mother, physical mother brought together, but along my journey it's about also how you bring experiences and how that shapes you. Particularly when it came to when my mother passed. I had to give a eulogy. I wanted to share that. When I was going through the process, I was sharing that with people, and some of the people in the audience and some of the people in the cast were sharing that with me.

When you have a publication like this, you have different people talking, everyone is doing their own thing. It's different. I think this is best summed up by the track *Little way Different* by Errol Dunkley. I used this for a project that was called *Best in the Book*. It was inspired by a publication of Lord Jonathan Sacks' called *Dignity of Difference: How to Avoid the Clash of Civilisations*. In the book, there are two arguments. One is moral; either the globalisation, politics and economics, or the other one deals with the difference, the sense of religion. Can you see the image of God with someone in your project, your race, your language? That's the nature of the book. The first stage of this project was for the Bradford Literature Festival 2015 and I am about to start on the second stage. The track itself says a lot, even though it's simple, it's about dance really. When you go and hear the sound system, the real sound system, it's from Jamaica, it's big boxes, DJ. The sound s ystem is the basis of reggae music. This is the basis of hip hop, rapping...

I love music. It can't be reggae music if you don't love it, period. Anybody who's into it hard core loves music and you must. You can't do it dance-wise otherwise. We did a show called *Runaway Diamonds*, based on the fact that Frederick Douglas came to Leeds to speak, and we based it around the fact that we did not speak American, we spoke from a Caribbean perspective. In terms of choreographic practice, you have to speak with your native tongue... as a member of the Caribbean.

REFERENCES

Sacks, J. (2004) *Dignity of Difference: How to Avoid the Clash of Civilisations. Continuum.*

Image Credit: David Hamilton in Phoenix Dance Theatre's Primal Impulse (1985). Photographer Terry Cryer Archives.

I FOUND DANCE THROUGH FLAMENCO

YINKA ESI GRAVES

INTRODUCTION

I am British and moved to Spain nine and a half years ago to learn Flamenco. I started learning Flamenco whilst at university (where I studied Art History). It is important for me to state that I have become a dancer through Flamenco. I wasn't a dancer before I decided to learn Flamenco.

I am not an academic. I am drawing conclusions and ideas based on my experience, where different cultures have influenced my choreographic voice and identity as a dancer. Unlike the dance world in the UK (of which I have to say I know very little), in the Flamenco world there is barely any dialogue around individual perspectives or clear positioning with regard to one's practice and choreographic voice, even less so from the question of identity. Never, in all the Flamenco festivals I have been to as an observer or even participant, have I seen a space for debate and discussion despite the wealth and increasing complexity surrounding questions of identity intrinsic to the art form. So, it is an honour for me to reflect upon these ideas.

Before I go into my specific dance journey I would like to give you a little bit of context around Flamenco dance and begin with this possibly overused Marcel Duchamp quote as a way in to understanding that Flamenco is as much about who watches it as who creates it. This is no doubt applicable to most performance arts on some level but, with Flamenco, it is from the very literal sense of the degree of audience participation.

This can range from no participation to *jaleos* (vocal participation) to actively getting up and dancing or singing. It denotes the specific cultural environment within which the act is taking place and it is through this relationship of shared or not shared cultural codes specific to Flamenco that I would like to talk about how culture and training influence choreographic vocabulary. From there, I can share my experience so far and how I have placed myself within this jigsaw puzzle.

> "The creative act is not performed by the artist alone; the spectator brings the work in contact with the external world by deciphering and interpreting its inner qualifications and thus adds his contribution to the creative act."
>
> *MARCEL DUCHAMP (1957)*

FLAMENCO

This is a very brief history of Flamenco. The term Flamenco is first used in 1847 to describe a more gypsy (jondo) version of the most popular form of music and dance of the time: bolero. From the beginning, it was used to relate to a more Spanish form of expression versus 'bolero' which was increasingly turning to French influence. The territorial aspect of Flamenco and its specific location is reflected in Andalucía, with important sites such as Cadiz, Seville, Malaga, despite expansion and involvement of artists from other parts of Andalucía and later Madrid. Flamenco is something that was primarily born and created in the south of Spain. Flamenco is not *Andalucían* folklore, or popular Andalucían music. It is created by a series of individuals, guitarists singers and dancers that have to be recognised as professionals (Gamboa, 2005; Nuñez, 2011).

In 1860, we start to see Café Cantantes, where the Flamenco that we know of today is born, the literal 'puesta en escena' placing on the stage of Flamenco. There were far fewer danceable 'palos' then. These came much later, in the twentieth century, where we see the form evolve based on the spaces it was performed in.

The rise of the Opera Flamenco as of the 1910s is where the idea of choreography starts to be thought of, and stars of the form are born and recognised: Antonía Merce La Argentina and Pastora Emperio, in dramatised operas, most famously Amor Brujo by Falla. From here much of the language and vocabulary that continues to be used is drawn. Vicente Escudero and Carmen Amaya also revolutionised the form. Escudero with his philosophy on dance and pioneering Siguiryas as a danceable style, and Amaya with her powerful footwork and turns, even dancing in trousers, completely changed how women could dance. They both remain important reference points in Flamenco dance today.

AESTHETICS, MYTHS AND STEREOTYPES

From the very beginning until now, intellectuals have been dedicated to defining what is and isn't Flamenco, in an attempt to establish a fixed identity for Flamenco and its artists. Figures such as Antonio Mairena and the study of Flamencología (the history and evolution of Flamenco) have helped define and create a notion of purity in the art form.

The Franco dictatorship also had a role in creating the aesthetic we all associate with Flamenco, which was and still is accentuated and used as symbol of Spanish expression, particularly as a tool in tourism as one of Spain's main cultural exports, at the hands, voices and feet of the country's Romani population (The Spanish Gypsies). This too has helped seal the widespread aesthetic around flamenco, it's creators and performers. Thinking back to the Duchamp quote, I've come to understand that despite this constructed homogeneity there exists a great complexity and tension between how flamenco artists are identified culturally and even ethnically, and the various spaces flamenco can be experienced in and consequently the varying ways in which audiences participate or don't with the art form. From within a community, at a national festivity, at a Peña, in a Tablao/ Café Cantante, on a theatre stage or in an international flamenco company; from the more local to the global, the question of the artist's cultural and ethnic background has varying weight. Specifically speaking, the question around being a Gypsy a non-Gypsy Spaniard (Payo) and in today's panorama I would even add a non-Spaniard.

SO HOW DO I FIT INTO THIS MIX?

Everything I have explained so far is really the context in which Flamenco exists as I understand it today. I knew none of this when I started taking classes at the age of 21. If I had I probably wouldn't have gone anywhere near it. It was the act of dancing and the music that somehow spoke to me, more than an image or an aesthetic. My love of Flamenco developed through dancing it, living it. Dance has been present throughout my life from Ballet, Jazz, Modern, West African Senegalese dance toAfro-Cuban dance. Once I moved to Spain indefinitely to continue learning Flamenco. It wasn't long before I came up against the question

It wasn't long before I came up against the question of what on earth I thought I was doing trying to become a Flamenco dancer. I clearly don't fit into the stereotype or aesthetic. This riddled my learning and experience with an underlying energy of doubt and not believing, as well as the question of appropriation here as an outsider coming to Flamenco. I thought maybe I shouldn't be coming here to 'steal' this art form (which I later discovered is reverse appropriation).

Yet the act of dancing is what I kept coming back to. My connection to the dance is what stopped me from giving up. Just over four years ago, after having been in Madrid for five years (where there is a focus on technique, speed and virtuosity), I decided to move to Seville. I really didn't like where my dancing was going, not only was I not good at it, but it really wasn't that which attracted me to Flamenco. I decided to move to Seville in an attempt to connect with the roots of the dance, wanting to get closer to the sensations that Flamenco provoked in me. I felt that there was where my voice could be nurtured.

Moving to Seville marked a real before and after on this journey so far. Not only because as a pupil, the style and focus of teaching is very different and is far more closely linked to the singing and the music and so is more alive, but also being in Seville, in the south of Spain, I started to discover a whole new world.

GURUMBÉ

After four months in Seville I get called one morning to shoot a "guajira" for a documentary. The documentary was called *Gurumbé: Canciones de tu Memoria Negra* (in English, Gurumbé: African Andalusian Memories), directed by Miguel Angel Rosales. I ended up becoming closely involved in the development of the film.

The film explored Spain's colonialist past and its involvement in the slave trade. Between the sixteenth and nineteenth centuries there was a Black population of up to fifteen per cent in Seville, it was as diverse as a modern-day London, if not more so. Gurumbé explored how the Black population influenced what later becomes Flamenco, through their rhythms and way of sharing the act of dancing.

This was a real game changer for me. So many ideas clarified in my mind and there was a real change in understanding the logic behind why I was drawn to Flamenco. Debunking the myths gave proof to my intuition, and having this affirmation gave me confidence in my right to want to be a flamenco dancer. I could create my own sense of belonging (despite there not traditionally being a space for me).

I suppose like the telling of history from a western perspective, it is fascinating to find yet another space within which everything is constructed through a homogenous lens. Flamenco as a Spanish form of expression, which is not at all questionable, this is site specific, but the question arises what is the site, who made up the Spanish population as Flamenco was being born?

IDENTITY REVEALED THROUGH PRACTICE

The freedom and limitation in Flamenco depends on which space you occupy and which people you identify as or with. I would fit into the foreigners' category, but being Black I sit on the peripheries of that too. When we keep in mind that whatever category you fall into there is a mimicking game of all trying to represent the same thing in an attempt to adhere to or belong to the widespread construct of what Flamenco is or more importantly who creates Flamenco.

Although more confusing, and perhaps more arduous, it feels like a privilege to be free to discover or allow my own identity to unfold. I'm never going to pretend to be a Spanish Gypsy. I can only ever be me, dual heritage Ghanaian and Jamaican British.

There is a huge contradiction that plagues Flamenco dance as I see it, speaking from where I stand today. As a form, I believe it is vast. It really allows for each individual to let their bodies interpret as is unique to them, so long as the very specific codes and music are understood, the idea of communicating with musicians and tapping into the management of energy that takes place in Flamenco. The form, free of all the socio-political context which I've spoken of, makes it an extremely open genre. But nothing exists without its socio-political context. What we find is that it is often the category that people identify with or as that determines their choreographic voice and even their vocabulary.

As the form evolves there are increasingly artists who are simply interested in exploring their unique voice. Opening the vocabulary that they employ, completely outside of the categories that Flamenco will accept as Flamenco. So more recently we hear of *'Flamenco contemporaneo'*, at the hands of incredible artists such as Juan Carlos Lérida, Israel Galvan, Andres Marín, Rocio Molina, to name the most important artists currently on the scene. However, in its essence to me, even if the vocabulary and invariably the aesthetics might be different, they are still dancing Flamenco. The unique relationship to rhythm and connection to 'palos' keeps it Flamenco in my eyes.

On a personal level, once I started taking my dancing more seriously, as in accepting that I too could be a flamenco dancer, I knew that I would have to create my own opportunities to develop and improve, in other words, to perform. Quite literally, getting into the spaces where Flamenco is performed, that I keep mentioning, as a foreigner, is very difficult. As an outsider that looks like one, it's even more difficult. So, in 2014 I got together with two other British born dancers, Magdalena Mannion and Noemí Luz, and we created our own company *dotdotdot* dance which really just arose out of a desire to perform with good musicians and get some proper experience.

Three years down the line, we self-produced three UK tours and we were invited to perform at Flamencos y Mestizos in Madrid which felt like a real honour to us! Although please note its name referring to those of mixed influences. Last year we were approached by the Lilian Baylis at Sadler's Wells to do a Wild Card and subsequently got programmed in SAMPLED 2017! We are currently developing a triple bill of work choreographed by each one of us, and collaborating with Tom Randle, opera composer and also Gillian Keith, singer on Los Nacimientos. It's quite incredible really when all we wanted was a chance to gain some experience!

In 2015, I started working with Asha Thomas on CLAY. This has been an incredible process for me. My first experience of creating a piece of work based on my reflections on Flamenco clearly relating to my identity as a Black woman. *I come to my body as a question* (2016-2017), which I choreographed for dotdotdot dance, was also an attempt to confront and challenge the only representation of a Black or 'mulatta' woman that has existed in the Flamenco genre, in one of its palos, the Guajira, where she is a celebrated sex symbol. This was a collaboration with the fantastic spoken word artist, Toni Stuart, where we played with her voice and words in juxtaposition and sometimes interweaving with the traditional flamenco song.

The process of creating and performing these works has completely changed my practice and also made me want to approach my dancing differently. For a very long time I have been preoccupied with the question of whether I could be a Flamenco dancer or not. In many ways I know this was very detrimental to my practice because somewhere in me there was always this sense that *'what was the point?'* since I was never really going to be a Flamenco dancer. So, in an odd way, I was quite passive with my learning, there were lots of things I could not do, and I thought that was fine, as I was never going to need it. I had this odd disjointed relationship with the practice that I was undergoing, and with this form of expression. On one level I felt drawn to it, yet on another level I was rejected by it. But overcoming that, my focus has become just about the dancing, my time in the studio, creating and in many ways relearning! At the moment, I am excited because I finally feel like I'm fully on board to discover why I came and have stayed with this particular form. I want to explore how my body wants to express itself, without feeling the pressure of defining it. That sort of definition to me has felt like a fight, and quite honestly a real waste of energy and focus. I always find the need to come back to the source, that unique energy that Flamenco produces and just keep it to that. The rest is beyond my control.

CONCLUSION

As I understand it, in an attempt to conserve Flamenco as it has been known, more energy is spent trying to define it according to what and who it includes and excludes, despite being a form that is born from the coming together of Spanish, Gypsy, West African, Moorish and Jewish cultures in Andalucía. This tension between those interested in limiting its boundaries and the very form itself, which is rich and complex in its diversity, has been the very tension that has shaped my dance experience so far. It has very much influenced the work I have made to date. The journey I am on has made me acutely aware of the need to create structures that need to redress understandings inherent in colonialism that have us wanting to partake in the same structures that have in the past excluded minorities. What I see as a false notion of diversity is currently being promoted as something to be aspired to. But the world, art, expression has always been diverse. It is the representation of it that isn't, hasn't been. For me it is important for us to remember this and for people to really feel their experience and perspective to be valid enough to be shared and given a place at the table.

REFERENCES

Duchamp, M. (1957). 'The Creative Act'. *Art News*, 56 (4).

Gamboa, J. M. (2005). *Una Historia Del Flamenco*. SLU Espasa Liberos

Nuñez, F. (2001). 'Flamencopolis' Available at: www.flamencopolis.com. (Accessed: 23 November 2017)

ART DANCE: AN UN-WINNABLE BATTLE

NORA CHIPAUMIRE

Over the past two decades I have sought to create work to challenge and negotiate the way Black African bodies are drawn, written, and read about in art-dance. Perhaps I have unwittingly implicated myself in an un-winnable battle. Race, gender and identity - an unholy trinity - have marked the work of artists, such as myself, who have been battling class systems and the colonial/imperial past for perhaps the past half century, if not longer! Is the engagement with the imperialist, capitalist beast - trench warfare - worth fighting? I have to say yes, and perhaps encourage those with the energy to continue in this war of artistic attrition.

At 51 years of age, having recovered my place within my native territory (Zimbabwe and Southern Africa), I feel the urgency to declaim this manifesto. I am enthused by my efforts to push the aesthetics of this war front. I have arrived at this juncture because I am curious as to how my work continues to be only partially read in terms of racial identity. My Zimbabwean-ness has become the preferred window through which critics have arrived at their (underwhelming) reading of the work. Otherness, another unfortunate artistic rubbish bin! A junkspace quagmire that is impossible to escape. Why have the critics focused less on the urgent utilisation of space, time, force (and the massive contribution regarding these efforts from artists of the global South)? Furthermore, where is the critique from the so-called global other? The West and non-West fail the artist with this myopia.

My work is beyond identity. It is beyond negritude, Black arts movements, Pan Africanisms, nationalisms. My work is to write new codes into, and to re-energise what has become a lethargic, boring, Western born, but dead art form: contemporary dance!

The poverty (i.e. the lack of art school education) that is assumed or implied by my colonial and imperialised past, is indeed the very regenerative power that art-dance needs. The hunger/austerity inherent in my work, introduces a way to make work - out of necessity and the imaginary, rather than out of leisure, pleasure, or art school induced labour production!

In my work...time is urgent: it is past, present and future, circular and linear at once. Energy is both physical and psychic at the same time. Physical space is nothing but an invitation to create the imaginary that is revolutionary, that is FREE! and possibly democratic. Bodies are human, and super human, intelligent, ruthless and pathetic; but they are humbled in the presence of God and other worlds unknown.

I am loyal to the lived experience and I believe that the personal truth which is well-imagined, or fictionalised, has universal potential. I believe in form with content. I believe in content within context. I believe in this choreographic utilitarianism. I trust the aesthetic of my raced, gendered, formerly colonised body; but I refuse to be reduced inexorably to the identity polemic. Art-dance can only thrive by the avant garde agency from outside the confines of its European past! Art dance needs the imaginary of the non-European body. In much the same way, the West needs the East's resources, labour, markets; and both need the South! The future is no longer in Paris, Berlin, London, or New York. The future is in the hands of urban youths in Kinshasa, Harare, Maputo. I want to walk with these youths into unimagined imaginaries.

Long live the dance.

GLOSSARY

By no means a conclusive guide this glossary provides an at-a-glance guide to further information regarding the practitioners, companies and techniques referenced by the contributors of this publication.

PRACTITIONERS AND COMPANIES

ABDUL, PAULA

Paula Abdul (1962-) is a singer, actor, choreographer and dancer. Abdul was a highly sought-after choreographer from music videos in the 1980s, including The Jacksons.

ABLOSO, AKUA

Akua Abloso is a lecturer in dance at the University of Ghana, focusing on the evolution and historical development of dance theatre in Ghana.

ACOGNY, GERMAINE

Germaine Acogny (1944-) is a Senegalese dancer and choreographer. She is renowned as the 'Mother of Contemporary African Dance' with her own technique, a hybrid between modern and traditional African techniques.

ACOSTA, CARLOS

Carol Acosta (1973-) is a Cuban ballet dancer. He has danced with English National Ballet, National Ballet of Cuba, Houston Ballet and American Ballet Theatre, and was a permanent member of The Royal Ballet (1998-2015).

ADAMS, PRECIOUS

Precious Adams is a First Artist with English National Ballet. Born in Michigan, USA she has trained at the Academy Princess Grace Monte Carlo, Monaco and Bolshoi Ballet Academy, Moscow.

AKINLEYE, ADESOLA

Adesola Akinleye began her career as a dancer with Dance Theatre of Harlem, she later established her own company DancingStrong, and is also a part-time senior lecturer at Middlesex University.

ALVIN AILEY DANCE THEATER

Founded in 1958 by Alvin Ailey, the company is credited with popularising modern dance and breaking barriers with its predominantly African-American company. Ailey's choreographic masterpiece *Revelations* (1960) is believed to be the most widely-seen modern dance work in the world.

ASTAFIEVIA, SERAFINA

Serafina Astafieva (1876–1934) was a Russian dancer and ballet teacher. After retiring from performing she opened the Russian Dancing Academy in London. Her pupils included Anton Dolin, Margot Fonteyn, Alicia Markova and Hermione Darnborough.

BAILEY, PEARL

Pearl Mae Bailey (1916-1990) was an American actress and singer. She appeared in Vaudeville and made her Broadway debut in *St. Louis Woman* (1946). She won a Tony Award for the title role in the all-Black production of Hello, Dolly! (1968).

BALLET BLACK

Founded in 2001 by Cassa Pancho, Ballet Black is a professional British ballet company for international dancers of Black and Asian descent, providing opportunities in classical ballet.

BALLETS RUSSE DE MONTE CARLO

Founded in 1932 in Monte-Carlo, the name Ballets Russes had been used by the impresario Serge Diaghilev for his company which revolutionised ballet in the twentieth century. After his death, Colonel W. De Basil took direction bringing new ballets and compositions to audiences.

BARNETT, SHELIA

Sheila Barnett (1928-2011) was a founder member of National Dance Theatre Company of Jamaica and the Jamaican School of Dance (later Edna Manley College of the Visual and Performing Arts).

BEARS-BAILEY, KIM

Kim Bears-Bailey is assistant artistic director of PHILADANCO, which she joined in 1981. She is a 1992 "Bessie" Award recipient, (The New York Dance and Performance Award), and represented PHILADANCO at the 1988 American Dance Festival as a soloist where she performed two works by Pearl Primus.

BECKFORD, ROBERT

Robert Beckford (1965-) is a British academic theologian born to Jamaican parents in Northampton, he is known for exploring debates around African and African Caribbean identity.

BÉJART BALLET LAUSANNE

Founded in 1987 by Maurice Béjart in Lausanne, Switzerland, and currently led by Gil Roman. Béjart's choreographic masterpiece includes *Bolero* (1960).

BIRMINGHAM ROYAL BALLET

Founded as the Sadler's Wells Theatre Ballet in 1946, under the direction of John Field. It remained at Sadler's Wells for many years, before relocating to Birmingham, UK in 1990, as the resident ballet company of the Birmingham Hippodrome.

BLACK DANCE DEVELOPMENT TRUST

Founded by Chester Morrison and Bob Ramdhanie in 1985 in Birmingham, UK to foster and promote the development of choreographic knowledge, understanding and appreciation of African People's dance, with summer schools to provide training.

BROWN, DAVID

David Brown is a dancer, teacher and choreographer, born in Jamaica. He studied dance at the Toronto Dance Theatre and performed with the Martha Graham Dance Company.

BULL, DEBORAH

Deborah Bull (1963 -) is an English dancer, writer and broadcaster, and former creative director of the Royal Opera House.

BUSH DAVIES SCHOOL OF THEATRE ARTS

Founded by Pauline Bush in Nottingham in 1914 it would become recognised as one of the foremost performing arts schools in the United Kingdom, until its closure in 1989.

CALLOWAY, CAB

Cabell "Cab" Calloway III (1907-1994) was an American jazz singer and bandleader. Associated with the Cotton Club in Harlem, his band *Cab Calloway* and *His Orchestra*, became famous for songs such as *Minnie the Moocher*, *St James Infirmary Blues* and *The Old Man of the Mountain*.

CECCHETTI CLASSICAL BALLET

Founded in 1922 by Maestro and Madame Cecchetti, the society was created to promote and support the art of classical ballet.

CHOW, MBYE

Mbye Chow is an actor, having performed with the National Drama Association in the Gambia, and at FESTAC in Nigeria.

CORONA THEATRE SCHOOL

(Formerly Corona Academy) was founded in 1957 by Rona Knight as a performing arts academy in West London.

DANCE THEATRE OF HARLEM   DANCE

Theatre of Harlem is an American professional ballet company and school based in Harlem, New York City. Founded in 1969 under the co-directorship of Arthur Mitchell and Karel Shook it was the first major Black classical ballet company.

DAO, THANG

Thang Dao is a freelance choreographer, teacher, and coach. Dao danced for the Stephen Petronio Company and the Metropolitan Opera until 2006, leaving to choreograph for Ballet Austin, Ballet Austin II, Ailey II, Ballet X and PHILADANCO.

DAVIS JR, SAMMY

Samuel George Davis Jr (1925 -1990) was an American singer, dancer, actor and comedian. Beginning his career in vaudeville, a star of stage and screen he appeared in his own TV variety show, Rat Pack film *Ocean's 11* (1933), and the Broadway hit *Mr Wonderful* (1954).

DAVIS, CHARLES RUDOLPH

Charles Rudolph Davis, also known as Baba Chuck Davis, (1937 - 2017) was an American dancer and choreographer whose work focused on traditional African dance in America. He was the founder of DanceAfrica, the Chuck Davis Dance Company and the African American Dance Ensemble.

DE LAVALLADE, CARMEN

Carmen De Lavallade (1931 -) is an American actress, dancer and choreographer. A lead dancer for Lester Horton Dance Theater (from 1949-1954), she has appeared on television and film including *Carmen Jones* (1954) and *Odds Against Tomorrow* (1959).

DEVLIN, GRAHAM

Graham Devlin is a creative artist, senior arts manager and cultural strategist. He was Deputy Secretary General and Acting Chief Executive of the Arts Council of England until 1999. As a stage director and writer, he ran the successful new writing and music-theatre company, Major Road.

DOWELL, ANTHONY

Anthony Dowell (1943-) is a British ballet dancer and former artistic director of the Royal Ballet. He is widely regarded as a *danseur noble*.

DUCHAMP, MARCEL

Henri-Robert-Marcel (1887-1968) was a French-American artist whose work is considered to be revolutionary for the development of conceptual art.

DYNOTT, SHEVELLE

Shevelle Dynott is a Black British ballet dancer, currently with the English National Ballet. He was discovered when 'Chance to Dance' visited his school in Brixton.

DZIKUNU, GEORGE

George Dzinkunu is a Ghanaian dancer and choreographer, founder of Adzido Pan African Dance Ensemble, presenting classical African tribal dance adapted for stage performance.

EDWARDS, BRENDA

Brenda Edwards was the first Black woman to work in a British ballet company when she joined English National Ballet. Brenda Edwards was also a company member of London Contemporary Dance Theatre and Martha Graham Dance Company.

EKOME DANCE COMPANY

Founded in 1972 by Barrington Anderson, in Bristol, UK. The initial approach was to adapt traditional African dances as a way of connecting to the Black British experience.

ELIE, MARK

Mark Elie is the artistic director of Portobello Dance based in North Kensington, offering opportunities for students from diverse backgrounds. Training at Rambert School of Ballet, he danced for Gulbenkian Dance Company, Dance Theatre of Harlem and Carol Straker Dance Company.

ELLIS, ANGELA

Angela Ellis (1920-2006) was a ballet teacher, dancer and director, her mother Marie Rambert formed Britain's first ballet company, while her father was the playwright Ashley Dukes. She founded Ballet Workshop in London, which gave Sunday night programmes of new works to find and nurture new talent.

ENGLISH NATIONAL BALLET

(Formerly London Festival Ballet) was founded in 1950 by Alicia Markova and Anton Dolin. Is one of the UK's four major ballet companies, and one of the foremost touring companies in Europe.

FELIX, JULIE

Julie Felix is a Black British ballet dancer, who danced with Dance Theatre of Harlem before returning to the UK to work with Birmingham Royal Ballet as a coach.

GALVÁN, ISRAEL

Israel Galván de los Reyes (1973-) is a Spanish flamenco dancer and choreographer, developing an avant-garde style of flamenco.

GARRETT-GLASSMAN, BRENDA

Brenda Garret-Glassman is a Black British ballet dancer. She trained at the Royal Ballet School and joined Dance Theatre of Harlem. Her other theatre credits *The Wiz and Kiss me Kate*.

GELLA, FRANCISCO

Francisco Gella is a professional dancer, choreographer, artistic director and educator, born in the Philippines. He is the artistic director for the Pioneering Youth Dance Festival.

GHANA DANCE ENSEMBLE

Founded in 1962, as an initiative from the Ghanaian's Government Institute of Arts and Culture and the Institute of African Studies.

GLASS, PHILIP

Philip Glass is an American composer. Glass' compositions have been described as minimal music, he has written numerous operas, musical theatre works and film scores, three of which have been nominated for Academy Awards.

GRAHAM, MARTHA

Martha Graham (1894 -1991) was an American dancer and choreographer, developing a contemporary dance technique that reshaped American dance. Martha Graham was the first dancer to perform at the White House and travel abroad as a cultural ambassador.

GREY, BERYL

Dame Beryl Elizabeth Grey, CH, DBE (1927-) is a retired English ballet dancer. In 1957, she became the first English dancer to appear as guest ballerina with the Kirov and Bolshoi Ballet and to appear with the Peking Ballet and Shanghai Company (with a Chinese partner) in 1964.

GUY, JACKIE

Carlton 'Jackie' Guy is a Jamaican dancer, choreographer and teacher. A member of the National Dance Theatre Company of Jamaica, and later the artistic director of Kokuma Dance Company.

HACKETT, JANE

Jane Hackett is the former director of the National Youth Dance Company and currently the Artistic Programmer and Producer for Creative Learning at Sadler's Wells.

HARRIS, RENNIE

Lorenzo Harris (1964 -) is a dancer, choreographer, artistic director and professor of hip hop dance. Harris formed the first and longest running hip hop dance touring company, Rennie Harris Puremovement in 1992.

HAYWARD, FRANCESCA

Francesca Hayward is a Principal of The Royal Ballet. Born in Nairobi to a Kenyan mother and British father, she trained at The Royal Ballet School and graduated into the company during the 2010/11 season, being promoted to First Artist in 2013, Soloist in 2014, First Soloist in 2015 and Principal in 2016.

HIGH SCHOOL OF PERFORMING ARTS

Founded in 1947, by Franklin J. Keller, a government funded school offering programmes in music and theatre arts in New York City.

HOLDER, CHRISTIAN

Christian Holder (1949 -) is a British-Trinidadian dancer, choreographer, actor, teacher, costume designer, writer, painter and singer, becoming a notable dancer for Jofferey Ballet Company in the 1970s.

HOLDER, GEOFFREY

Geoffrey Lamont Holder (1930-2014) was a Trinidadian-American actor, dancer, choreographer, and director. His movie career began with British film *All Night Long* (1962) and he star red as Baron Samedi in *Live and Let Die* (1973), he won two Tony Awards for direction and costume design of The Wiz (1975).

HUGGINS, CHRISTOPHER L.

Christopher L. Huggins is a former member of Alvin Ailey American Dance Theater, he is recipient of the Alvin Ailey Award for Best Choreography from the Black Theater Alliance in Chicago for *Enemy Behind the Gates* (2002) and *Pyrokinesis* (2008).

INTERNATIONAL ASSOCIATION OF BLACKS IN DANCE

International Association of Blacks in Dance (IABD) Founded in 1991, the association responds to and initiates dialogue around issues that impact on the Black dance community, with a network, newsletter, published papers and annual conference.

IPI TOMBI

A 1974 musical by South African Bertha Egnos Godfrey and her daughter Gail Lakier, using pastiches of a variety of South African indigenous musical styles. It won the 1976 Laurence Oliver Award for Best New Musical.

JAFFRAY, DARRYL

Darryl Jaffray is the Royal Ballet's head of education, credited with starting the 'Chance to Dance' programme to find promising dancers who haven't had the opportunity for formal dance training.

JAMAICAN SCHOOL OF DANCE

Now the Edna Manley College of the Visual and Performing Arts. Was founded in 1950, to provide training in the arts in Jamaica.

JAMES, ADAM

Adam James is a Black British dancer. After training with the Royal Academy, he later became a dancer for Dance Theater of Harlem.

JOHNSON LOUIS

Louis Johnson (1930 -) is a director and choreographer. He provided choreography for *Black Nativity* by Langston Hughes, and received acclaim for choreographing operas performed by the New York Metropolitan Opera including *La Giaconda and Aida*, and films *Cotton Comes to Harlem* (1970) and *The Wiz* (1978).

JOHNSON, CHRISTINA

Christina Johnson is a dancer, ballet master and rehearsal director. A former member of Boston Ballet and Dance Theatre of Harlem, she is currently the rehearsal director for Complexions Contemporary Ballet.

JOHNSON, LINTON KWESI

Linton Kwesi Johnsn (1952-) is a Jamaican-British dub poet. Acclaimed for his poetry dealing with the African Caribbean experience, with a political edge.

KHAN, AKRAM

Akram Kahn (1974 -) is British dancer and choreographer of Bangladeshi descent, his training is rooted in classical kathak and contemporary dance.

KHAN, NASEEM

Naseem Kahn (1939 - 2017) was a British journalist, activist, cultural historian and educator of Indian-German heritage. Kahn was instrumental in initiating debate and policy change about cultural diversity with her reports including *The Arts Britain Ignores* (1979).

KIMMEL CENTER FOR THE PERFORMING ARTS

The Kimmel Center is a world-class performing arts centre based in Philadelphia that engages and serves a broad audience through diverse programming, arts education, and community outreach.

LADZEPKO, C.K.

C.K. Ladzepko is a performer, choreographer and composer and is currently the director of African music programme at the University of California in Berkeley.

LANZEL AFRICAN ARTS

Founded by Chester Morrison in Wolverhampton, UK in 1975, the company drew upon traditional African rhythms and patterns.

LEGAT SCHOOL OF CONTEMPORARY DANCE AND BALLET

Founded in 1923 by Russian ballet dancers Nicolai and Nadine Legat, it became the first British ballet boarding school, focusing initially on Russian ballet, before branching out into contemporary techniques.

LÉRIDA, JUAN CARLOS

Juan Carlos Lérida is a dancer, choreographer and instructor of flamenco. His work includes *Flamenco Empirico* (2009), El *Aprendizaje* (2011) and *Al Baile* (2014)

LES BALLETS NÈGRES

Founded in London in 1946 by Berto Pasuka and Richie Riley, Les Ballets Nègres was Britain's first Black dance company. The company drew inspiration African Caribbean folk tales and rituals.

LEWIS, PATRICK

Patrick Lewis danced with the Cullberg Ballet and Royal Swedish Ballet before joining the English National Ballet in 1986 as a soloist. He currently teaches at the Royal Academy of Dance and Royal Ballet.

MAIRENA, ANTONIO

Antonio Cruz Garcia (1909 -1983) was a Spanish musician credited with his attempts to revive lost styles of "pure" flamenco music, publishing several books and articles on flamenco history

MAJEWSKI, RICHARD

Richard Majewski is a Black Britsh dancer. He joined Bejart Ballet in Switzerland in 1970, performing with the company for seven years.

MARÍN, ANDRES

Andres Marin (1843-1896) was a Spanish tenor who belonged to the choir of Teatro Real.

MCCARTHY-BROWN, NYAMA

Nyama McCarthy-Brown is an assistant professor of contemporary dance at Indiana University, her research focuses on the visceral experience of culture through movement.

MITCHELL, ARTHUR

Arthur Mitchell (1934 -) is an African-American dancer and choreographer who created a training school and the first African-American classical ballet company, Dance Theatre of Harlem. He is a recipient of the United States National Medal of Arts.

MOLINA, ROCIO

Rocio Molina Cruz (1984 -) is a Spanish dancer and choreographer, in 2010 she was awarded the National Dance Prize by the Ministry of Culture of Spain.

MOOR, MICHAEL

Michael Moor is a British dancer and dance educator. A company member of Dance Theatre of Harlem, he also appeared in Octopussy (1983) and The Living Daylights (1987).

MOSAVAL, JOHAAR

Johaar Mosaval (1928 -) is a retired South African ballet dancer who rose to prominence as a principal dancer with England's Royal Ballet. He was among the first dancers from ethnic minority backgrounds to perform major roles with an internationally known ballet company during the 1960s.

NATIONAL ENDOWMENT FOR THE ARTS

Established by the United States Congress in 1965, the National Endowment for the Arts is an independent federal agency which gives funding for the arts.

NETTLEFORD, REX

Ralston Milton 'Rex' Nettleford (1933-2010) was a Jamaican scholar, social critic and choreographer. He co-founded the National Dance Theatre Company of Jamaica and director of the University Singers of the University of the West Indies.

NEW YORK CITY BALLET COMPANY

Founded in 1948 by George Balanchine and Lincoln Kirstein, with Jerome Robbins being considered one of the company's founding choreographers. The company has the largest repertoire of any American ballet company.

NGUBANE, ELLIOTT

Elliott Ngubane is a South African actor based in London, known for *Scene* (1968) and *Shaka Zulu* (1986).

NII YARTEY, FRANCIS

Francis Nii Yartey (1946 - 2015) was the artistic director and choreographer of the Ghana Dance Ensemble, University of Ghana. An associate professor of the Institute of African Studies, University of Ghana, his research focused on the creation and development of Contemporary African Dance in Ghana.

NKETIA, J.H.

Joseph Hanson Kwabena Nketia (1921-) is a Ghanaian ethnomusicologist and composer, and is one of the most published and best-known experts in African music and aesthetics.

NKRUMAH, KWAME

Kwame Nkrumah (1909-1972) was a Ghanaian politician and revolutionary. The first prime minister and president of Ghana, he was an influential advocate of Pan-Africanism.

NORTHCOTE, ANNA

Anna Northcote (1907-1988) also known as Anna Severskaya was an English dancer and teacher who trained several dancers including Berto Pasuka.

NUREYEV, RUDOLF

Rudolf Khametovich Nureyev (1938 - 1993) was a Russian ballet dancer and choreographer. After defecting from the Soviet Union in 1961, her went on to dance with The Royal Ballet and was director of the Paris Opera Ballet.

ODEDRA, AAKASH

Aakash Odedra is a dancer and choreographer from Birmingham, UK and now based in Leicester, UK with a background in Kathak and Bharat Natyam, with influences from contemporary dance and theatre. His credits include James Brown: *Get on the Good Foot* (2013) and *Sukanya* (2017).

OPOKU, ALBERT MAWERE

Albert Mawere Opoku (1915 - 2002) was a Ghanaian choreographer, dancer, artist and educator, and one of the founders of the Ghana Dance Ensemble.

PANCHO, CASSA

Cassa Pancho (1978 -) is the founder and artistic director of Ballet Black. Of Dual heritage her parents are Trinidadian and British. She studied ballet at the Royal Academy.

PANTON, DARREN

Darren Panton is a dancer and choreographer, trained at the Royal Ballet School he has worked with the Royal Ballet, Birmingham Royal Ballet, BBC and Channel 4.

PASUKA, BERTO

Berto Pasuka, born Wilbert Passerley (1911 - 1963) was a Jamaican dancer and choreographer. Inspired to take Black dance to new audiences, he moved to London in 1939. In the 1940s he founded Les Ballet Negres, with fellow Jamaican dancer Richie Riley.

PERRY, RONALD

Ronald Perry began his professional career with Dance Theatre of Harlem. In 1990, he and Christina Johnson became the first Black dancers to appear with the Royal Ballet since the departure of Johaar Mosaval. He later joined Béjart Ballet.

PHILADANCO - THE PHILADELPHIA DANCE COMPANY

Founded in 1970 by Joan Myers Brown, PHILADANCO is celebrated for its innovation, creativity and preservation of predominantly African-American traditions in dance with a legacy of breaking barriers and building bridges across cultural divides.

PHILADELPHIA SCHOOL OF DANCE ARTS

Founded by Joan Myers Brown in 1960, to provide opportunities for primarily African American students, the school offers a high level of dance training and technique.

PHOENIX DANCE THEATRE

(Formally Phoenix Dance Company) was founded in 1981, in Harehills, Leeds by David Hamilton, Donald Edwards and Vilmore James. The company is now one of Britain's leading contemporary dance companies, under the direction of Sharon Watson.

POMARE, ELEO

Eleo Pomare (1937- 2008) was a Colombian-American modern dance choreographer known for his politically charged productions depicting the Black experience, his works include *Missa Luba* (1965), *Blues for the Jungle* (1966) and *Narcissus Rising* (1968).

POWELL, STEPHANIE

Stephanie Marie Powell is a tenured Professor of Dance at Long Beach City College in Southern California. Her stage and screen credits include *The Lion King*, *The Grammy's* and the *Jay Leno Show*.

PRIMUS, PEARL

Pearl Eileen Primus (1919 -1994) was a dancer, choreographer and anthropologist, who played an integral role in promoting African dance as an art form worthy of study and performance. Primus' choreography includes a piece set to Langston Hughes's famous poem *The Negro Speaks of Rivers* (1944).

RICKETTS, PATSY

Patricia Judith Maryla Ricketts is a dancer and dance educator, having danced with the National Dance Theatre Company of Jamaica, Martha Graham Company and Dance Theatre of Harlem.

RILEY, RICHARD

Richard 'Richie' Theopbilus Riley was a co-founder of Les Ballet Nègres and performing partner to Pasuka. A key influence was Marcus Mosiah Garvey's perspective that culture and arts were integral to Jamaican assertiveness.

RJC DANCE

Founded in 1993 by Edward Lynch, Donald Edwards and David Hamilton, the Black British company focus on reggae, jazz and contemporary dance influences.

ROGERS, ROD

Rod Rogers (1912 - 1983) was a modern dance choreographer known for his work reflecting social themes grown out of his experiences as an African-American, including *Crime* (1945), *Youth Aflame* (1944) and *Embraceable You* (1948).

ROJO, TAMARA

Tamara Rojo (1974 -) is a Spanish ballet dancer and artistic director of the English National Ballet, commissioning new contemporary work for the company and developing a partnership with Sadler's Wells.

ROYAL BALLET SCHOOL

The Royal Ballet School was founded in 1926, and is a world-renowned centre of classical ballet training dancers for The Royal Ballet (based at the Royal Opera House in London) and Birmingham Royal Ballet.

SEKYI, RACHEL

Rachel Sekyi is a dancer and dance educator for Dance Theatre of Harlem, she trained at Italia Conti Academy of Theatre Arts in London.

SHOOK, KAREL

Karel Shook (1920 — 1985) was an internationally renowned ballet master, author and co-founder of the Dance Theater of Harlem. Mr. Shook, who was white, was one of the few ballet masters in the 1950s who taught and encouraged Black ballet dancers. Among his students were Arthur Mitchell, Alvin Ailey, Carmen de Lavallade and Geoffrey Holder.

SINGLETON, TYRONE

Tyrone Singleton trained at the Arts Educational School in Tring and the Royal Ballet School and joined in 2003; but was Principal, 2013. He has made guest appearances: Faster and Carmina Burana with the National Ballet of Japan.

SONNTAG, DOUGLAS

Douglas Sonntag is the former general manager for Repertory Dance Theatre in Salt Lake City, and former director of the National Endowment for the Arts.

SOWAH, NII

Nii Kwei Sowah is a dancer, actor, choreographer, artistic director and lecturer at the University of Ghana, his research interests include national identity.

SOYINKA AJAYI, OMOFOLABO

Omofolabo Ajaui-Soyinka is an interdisciplinary scholar, her teaching, research publications and creative works encompass theatre, performance, literary and gender studies, including the critical theories that inform them.

SPALDING, MALACHI

Malachi Spaulding trained at the Northern School of Contemporary Dance and Ballet Rambert, and is a former member of the renowned African dance company Irie Dance Theatre.

SPRINGER, JEANETTE

Jeanette Springer is the founder of the Shades of Black Dance Company. Formed in 1972, the company specialise in Caribbean folk dance.

STRAKER, CAROL

Carol Straker (1961 -) is a Black British dancer, performing with Dance Theatre of Harlem, Martha Graham Ensemble and Alvin Ailey American Dance Theatre. She founded the Carol Straker Dance Company (1988-2001) who provided opportunities to Black dancers who were not accepted by the English National Ballet and The Royal Ballet.

THE 291 CLUB

The 291 Club was an Urban Talent Show popular in the 1990s, recorded live from the Hackney Empire.

THE JOFFREY BALLET

Founded in 1956, by Robert Joffrey and Gerald Arpino, the company has become renowned for its original ballets. It was the first dance company to perform at the White House, appear on American television and create a ballet set to rock music.

TIEROU, ALPHONSE

Alphonse Tierou is an African dancer, researcher and choreographer. Originally from the Ivory Coast, he has theorised and codified African dance, defining an African dance vocabulary with ten basic moves common to all African cultures.

UNDERWOOD, ERIC

Eric Underwood is a former Soloist of The Royal Ballet (2006 - 2017). Born in the USA, he has also danced with Dance Theatre of Harlem and American Ballet Theatre in 2003.

WALLACE, NOEL

Noel Wallace made British ballet history as the English National Ballet's first Black male dancer in the 1980s. Noel also danced with the Houston Ballet and Béjart Ballet.

WEBB, SAMANTHA

Samantha Webb (Binah) is a Back British dancer who trained with London School of Contemporary Dance, and Dance Theatre of Harlem.

WELSH ASANTE, KARIAMU

Kariamu Welsh Asante is Director of the Institute for African Dance Research and Performance and the author of numerous books including: *Zimbabwe Dance: Rhythmic Forces, Ancestral Voices and an Aesthetic Analysis and Umfundalai: An African Dance Technique.*

WILLIAMS, EVAN

Evan Williams is a Black British Dancer and was the first Black dancer to be accepted by the Birmingham Royal Ballet's corps de ballet in 1991.

WYE, JACOB

Jacob Wye is a Black British dancer. Currently with Rambert, he is a previous member of Ballet Black and is also a music producer for M22 Movement Lab.

ZOLLAR, JAWOLE WILLA JO

Jawole Willa Jo Zollar (1950 -) is a dancer, teacher and choreographer. In 1984, Jawole founded Urban Bush Women (UBW), a performance ensemble dedicated to exploring the use of cultural expression as a catalyst for social change.

TECHNIQUES

AGBADZA

Aqbadza is an Ewe music and dance that evolved from the times of war into a very popular recreational dance. It is originally done by the Ewe people of the Volta Region of Ghana, particularly during the Hogbetsotso Festival, a celebration by the Anlo Ewe people. This dance is also seen in present-day Togo and Benin.

BOLERO

Bolero is a genre of slow-tempo Latin music and its associated dance. There are Spanish and Cuban forms which are both significant and which have separate origins.

CAFÉ CANTANTES

Café Cantates are Spanish entertainment venues, essentially a café with performance area for light entertainment, frequently flamenco tablaos.

CONTEMPORARY REGGAE

Reggae is a genre of music and associated dance, strongly influenced by mento, a style of Jamaica folk music, and American jazz, rhythm and blues, growing out of ska and rocksteady. The music nourished dance culture, and choreographers have incorporated this with contemporary techniques to create a unique movement style.

DANCEHALL

Dancehall is a genre of Jamaican popular music and subculture that originated in the late 1970s. Initially, dancehall was a sparser version of reggae than the roots style, faster rhythms characterised the genre with digital developments in the 1980s. It is a place where various people from different walks of life can come together to dance.

EMBODIOLOGY©

Embodiology is an improvisation-as-performance—method developed by Sheron Wray. It takes its cues from West Africa's aesthetics and is applied to create contemporary dance performance. Adapting six structuring principles identified in Ewe and Yoruba dance and music performance facilitates unique streams of creativity. At its core, it explores the complexity of rhythm and the relationship of rhythm to spoken language and observes deep listening as the first order of the creative process.

FLAMENCO CONTEMPORANEO

Flamenco contemporeano (literally Contemporary Flamenco) is the fusion of flamenco and contemporary dance.

FLAMENCOLOGÍA

Flamencología is the academic discipline of Flamenco arts. It combines research, documentation, and other techniques to achieve the dissemination and preservation of the art form.

GRAHAM TECHNIQUE

Graham technique is widely regarded as the first codified modern dance technique, developed by Martha Graham. The technique is based on opposition between contraction and release, the movement of the torso around the axis of the spine and dramatic expressive qualities.

GULE WAMKULU

Gule Wamkulu was a ritual dance practiced among the Chewa in Malawi, Zambia and Mozambique. It was performed by members of the secret society, the Nyau brotherhood. Nyau members still are responsible for the initiation of young men into adulthood, and for the performance of the Gule Wamkulu at the end of the initiation procedure, celebrating the young men's integration into adult society. It can also be seen at weddings, funerals, and the installation or the death of a chief. On these occasions, the Nyau dancers wear costumes and masks made of wood and straw, representing a great variety of characters, such as wild animals and spirits.

HORTON TECHNIQUE

A contemporary dance technique developed by Lester Horton, based on Native American dances, which focuses on warming up the body quickly, with clearly defined shapes and movement segue. Lester Horton was also one of the first American choreographers to insist on racial integration in his company.

JALEOS

Jaleos are a chorus in flamenco in which dancers and the singer clap. More particularly, in flamenco jaleo includes words of encouragement called out to the performers, as individuals or as a group, as well as hand-clapping.

L'ANTECH

L'Antech is a system of dance developed by L'Antoinette Stines, combining indigenous and traditional Caribbean dance with techniques borrowed from other modern contemporary dance styles and classical ballet.

LIKISHI

Likishi is a dance common to the Lunda, Lwena, Luvale and Luchazi tribes in Angola and Zambia. Danced at ceremonies, it has many variations according to the tribe and occasion.

MYAL

Myal (also mayaal) is the physical representation of power. It is an African Jamaican form of divination and a ritual dance by which spirit mediums drew on the power of ancestors to heal and to alleviate misfortune ascribed to the jealousy, greed, and enmity of others.

NYABINGHI

Nyabhinghi is distinctive dancing, drumming and chanting specific to Rastafari. The drumming features three kinds of drums: bass, which strikes loud on the first beat and softly on the third; the middle-pitched funde which plays a regular one-two beat and the akete (also known as the repeater) which plays an improvised syncopation. The other drums keep regular rhythms while the akete players solo in the form of a conversation. Its rhythms are the basis of Reggae music, ska and rock steady.

PALO

Palo (or cante) is the name given in flamenco for the different traditional musical forms.

PUESTA EN ESCENA'

Puesta en escena' (from the French Mise-en-scène) refers to the global design aspects of a scenic production.

VIMBUZA

Vimbuza is a healing dance popular among the Tumbuka people living in northern Malawi. It is an important manifestation of the ng'oma, a healing tradition found throughout Bantu-speaking Africa. Ng'oma, meaning "drums of affliction". Women and children of the village form a circle around the patient, who slowly enters into a trance, and sing to call helping spirits. The only men taking part are those who beat spirit-specific drum rhythms and, in some cases, a male healer. Singing and drumming combine to create a powerful experience, providing a space for patients to "dance their disease".

YANVALOU

Yanvalou (also Yanvalu, Yanvaloo) is a Haitian dance in which the focus is undulation of the spinal column, and represents the snake god Damballa.

BIOGRAPHIES

FRANCIS ANGOL

Francis Angol is the Artistic Director of Movement Angol dance, a Somatics Movement Educator, performer, choreographer and associate tutor in dance at the University of Surrey. His former role was that of Assistant Artistic Director and Choreographer for Badejo Arts, Britain's former ground-breaking contemporary African dance company, under the directorship of Peter Badejo, OBE. At present, Francis is one of Britain's few dance artists that produces work under the genre definition of contemporary African dance, within the wider context of health and wellbeing with the development of his therapeutic movement practice, 'BodyRhythms'. In addition to running his own company, Francis also holds the position of Director of Dance at Islington Arts Factory, North London's creative hub for art, music and dance.

DELIA BARKER

Delia is the Programmes Director at the Roundhouse, London. Until recently she was the Director of English National Ballet School. Additionally, Delia has been working as an independent consultant specialising in business development within the performing arts sector, working with Drake Music, Boy Blue Entertainment, Theatre Peckham and StopGap Dance Company. She is the Chair of Studio Wayne McGregor and a sitting member of the Green Spring Trust.

Delia spent several years as ACE Senior Officer for Dance and was recently accredited as Organisational Development practitioner with NTL Institute for Applied Behavioural Science.

SANDIE BOURNE

Sandie Bourne is taking a PhD in Dance Studies at Roehampton University. Her research has captured interest and she has presented papers at the University of Bedfordshire, ADAD, Pavilion Dance South West, London Metropolitan University and was a panellist for 'Dance and the Creative Case' which was part of the Arts Council's 'Decibel' performing arts conference on diversity and equality in Manchester, September 2011. She trained 3 years as a dancer at London Studio Centre, has a BA in Performing Arts, Major in Dance from Middlesex University and a MA in Dance Studies from Surrey University.

PAWLET BROOKES

Pawlet is the Founder and Executive Artistic Director of Serendipity, a diversity led organisation that initiated and produces LDIF (Let's Dance International Frontiers), an annual festival in Leicester since 2011, and also delivers each year a Black History Month programme for Leicester as well as other projects and publications. Pawlet is an accomplished and experienced senior manager and producer who has been at the heart of the development of Black arts centres, from the Nia Centre (Manchester) to the Artistic Director of Peepul Centre (Leicester) and Chief Executive of Rich Mix (London). She has also been the Arts Council assessor for a number of Black arts capital projects.

JOAN MYERS BROWN

Joan Myers Brown founded the Philadelphia School of Dance Arts in 1960, offering African American dancers access to professional training which traditional schools would deny them. In 1970 she founded PHILADANCO – The Philadelphia Dance Company. She initiated the Smithonian Institution's International Conference for Black Dance Companies in 1988 and the International Association of Blacks in Dance (IABD) in 1991. Joan Myers Brown was honoured in the 2012 National Medal of the Arts, the highest civic honour in the USA for excellence in the arts. President Barack Obama presented the prestigious honour at a ceremony that took place in July 2013 at the White House. Most recently Joan Myers Brown has been honoured by the Dance Heritage Coalition as one of America's Irreplaceable Dance Treasures.

NORA CHIPAUMIRE

Born in Mutare, Zimbabwe and based in New York, Nora Chipaumire has been challenging and embracing stereotypes of Africa and the black performing body, art and aesthetic. She is a graduate of the University of Zimbabwe's School of Law and holds a M.A. in Dance and M.F.A. in Choreography and Performance from Mills College. She has studied dance in Africa, Cuba, Jamaica and the U.S.A. and has performed internationally in France, Italy, Japan, Senegal, Zimbabwe and many other places. Chipaumire is a three-time New York Dance and Performance (aka "Bessie") Awardee: in 2014 for the revival of her solo dark swan set as an ensemble piece on Urban Bush Women (UBW), in 2008 for her dance-theatre work, Chimurenga, and in 2007 for her body of work with UBW, where she was a featured performer for six years and Associate Artistic Director (2007-2008).

YINKA ESI GRAVES

Yinka is a British Flamenco dancer. Her dance journey has taken her from ballet, jazz and African Cuban dancing at a young age, to studying Flamenco in Spain in the world-renowned school Amor de Dios with artists such as La Lupi, Manuel Reyes and Pepa Molina. She has performed with Santiago de Cuba's Folklore dance troupe, Ikache, and Cristobal Reyes' Flamenco Company at the Royal Albert Hall and Teatro Calderon in Madrid. Since 2011 Yinka has been performing in tablaos and venues such as Candela (Madrid), Upstairs at Ronnie Scotts (London) and La Sala Zero (Seville). Yinka co-founded dotdotdot dance alongside two other flamenco dancers in 2014. In 2015 Yinka began working with former principal Alvin Ailey dancer Asha Thomas on CLAY.

DAVID HAMILTON

David Hamilton is a reggae contemporary dancer, teacher, director/producer of Dance Theatre, performance poet and dance researcher. He was one of the the founders of Phoenix Dance Theatre, founder member of R J C Dance and founder of Reggeyieshun Dance Theatre. His work has been celebrated across the world, including UK, Spain, Trinidad, Jamaica, Australia and South Africa.

TERRY OFOSU

Terry Bright Kweku Ofosu is former National Dance Champion of Ghana and Assistant Lecturer at the Department of Dance Studies, University of Ghana, and has been teaching since January 2011. He is currently a fulltime PhD candidate at the Institute of African Studies, University of Ghana. Ofosu's areas of interest are 'popular dance and its intersection with traditional dance' and also 'dance, film and 3D animation.' He is the originator of popular dance techniques at the University of Ghana, Legon and his extensive research into Azonto dance and Alkayida makes him an authority of popular dance research in Ghana.

'H' PATTEN

'H' Patten is the Artistic Director of Koromanti Arts and 'H' Patten Dance Theatre Co. An experienced choreographer, filmmaker, visual artist, storyteller, author and performer, 'H' has developed an international reputation in African and Caribbean arts over the past 35 years. He is the recipient of several awards including the ADAD Trailblazer Fellowship (2010) and the Jamaican High Commission Fiftieth Anniversary Award for services in the field of Arts, Culture and Entertainment (2012). He has developed his own 'Korotech' dance technique, using both traditional and popular movement vocabulary from out of the African and Caribbean dance idiom. In 2012 'H' embarked on his PhD research on the topic; Dancehall: A Spiritual Corporeal Practice in Jamaican Dance, at Canterbury Christ Church University.

KENRICK 'H2O' SANDY

Born in East London, Kenrick 'H2O' Sandy is Co-founder and Co-Artistic Director of Boy Blue Entertainment and Associate Artist at the Barbican, London. Kenrick has created choreography for artists as diverse as Rita Ora, Plan B, Stooshe, Dizzee Rascal and Alexandra Burke and has worked additionally with Nike, Adidas and Asos. For the stage, Kenrick choreographed *Blak Whyte Gray* (2017) which is nominated in the Best New Dance Production category in the 2017 Olivier Awards. Kenrick worked alongside director Danny Boyle as choreographer for the *Frankie and June say thanks Tim...* for the London 2012 Olympic Games Opening Ceremony, which won the Evening Standard's Beyond Theatre Award. In January 2017, Kenrick was awarded an MBE for services to dance and the community.

SHERON WRAY

Associate Professor of Dance at UCL, Sheron describes herself as a 'Neo-African *Performance Architect*'. Receiving her PhD from the University of Surrey her interdisciplinary scholarship engages with dance, music, spiritual and community-held knowledge which evolved into her praxis of *Embodiology®*. Sheron's foundation is in dance performance and in the UK she was a member of both London Contemporary Dance Theatre and Rambert Dance Company between 1988 and 2001. Sheron is widely known for her role as the leading performer and legal custodian of *Harmonica Breakdown* (1938), choreographed by Jane Dudley. In 2013 she re-launched JazzXchange in the USA and, as a result of her NESTA fellowship intersect in her concept of digitally enabled improvisation, produced the award-winning *Texterritory*, created in collaboration with Fleeta Siegel.

Image Credit: Eric Underwood. Photographer Rick Guest / East